ASHEVILLE

presented to:

RIVERBEND BOOKS

A division of BOOKHOUSE GROUP, INC.

ASHEVILLE

a photographic portrait

ASHEVILLE
a photographic portrait

EDITOR .... Rob Levin
PUBLISHER.. Barry Levin
ASSOCIATE PUBLISHER .... Bob Sadoski
COMMUNITY LIAISON .... Jane Anderson
CHIEF OPERATING OFFICER .... Renée Peyton
DESIGN MANAGER .... Ann Fowler
ASSOCIATE EDITOR .... Rena Distasio
PROJECT DIRECTOR .... Muriel Diguette
PHOTO EDITORS .... Ann Fowler, Jill Dible
WRITERS .... Kimberly DeMeza, Rena Distasio,
....Grace Hawthorne, Amy Meadows, Regina Roths, Gail Snyder
COPY EDITOR .... Bob Land
BOOK DESIGN .... Compòz Design
JACKET DESIGN .... Jill Dible
PREPRESS .... Vickie Berdanis
PHOTOGRAPHERS .... Tim Barnwell, Thomas S. England,
.... Scott Indermaur, Mario Morgado, Rod Reilly, Alan Weiner

Copyright © 2007 by Bookhouse Group, Inc.
Printed and bound in China

RIVERBEND BOOKS
A division of BOOKHOUSE GROUP, INC.

Published by Riverbend Books
an Imprint of Bookhouse Group, Inc.
818 Marietta Street, NW
Atlanta, Georgia 30318
www.riverbendbooks.net
404.885.9515

Asheville : a photographic portrait / [editor, Rob Levin].
p. cm. ISBN 978-1-883987-32-9
1. Asheville (N.C.)—Pictorial works. 2. Asheville (N.C.)—Description and travel.
3. Asheville (N.C.)—Social life and customs. 4. Asheville (N.C.)—Economic conditions.
5. Business enterprises—North Carolina—Asheville. I. Levin, Rob, 1955-
F264.A8A76 2007
975.6'88—dc22
2007030022

T

The longest river in North Carolina and third-oldest river in the world, the French Broad River offers unparalleled kayaking for people of all ages and experience levels. With wide shorelines and slow-moving waters, the historic waterway takes adventurers through some of the most beautiful landscapes in Western North Carolina. As kayakers gently traverse the river, they move seamlessly through the majestic mountains of the area and experience a truly one-of-a-kind trip, during which they enjoy the kind of peace and solitude that only Mother Nature can provide. And just like Bob Fay, pictured here kayaking on a cool spring morning, everyone can become one with the world around them by putting in at the confluence of the West and North forks of the famous French Broad River.

(left page)

A stroll through historic Pack Square in downtown Asheville becomes a euphonious experience when one is greeted by the mellifluous sounds of fiddler Darin Gentry and guitar picker Christopher Casbarro. The fun local flavor offered up by such delightful acts captivates residents and visitors and truly adds to the charm for which Asheville is known. Whether it's bluegrass on the corner or an a cappella song down the street, taking a tour of one of the city's most celebrated areas is music to everyone's ears.

(right page)

It started out as the all-volunteer Asheville Little Symphony in 1958, performing in schools and churches. Today the Asheville Symphony operates on a budget of almost $1 million with an eighty- to one-hundred-member orchestra. Led by musical director and conductor Daniel Meyer, the symphony presents seven full concerts per year in the Thomas Wolfe Auditorium. The programs balance old favorites and more recent works. In addition to the regular subscription series, audiences always look forward to the Holiday Pops performances.

photo by mario morgado

photo by mario morgado

photo by alan s. weiner

CONTENTS

photo by rod reilly

photo by rod reilly

photo by scott indermaur

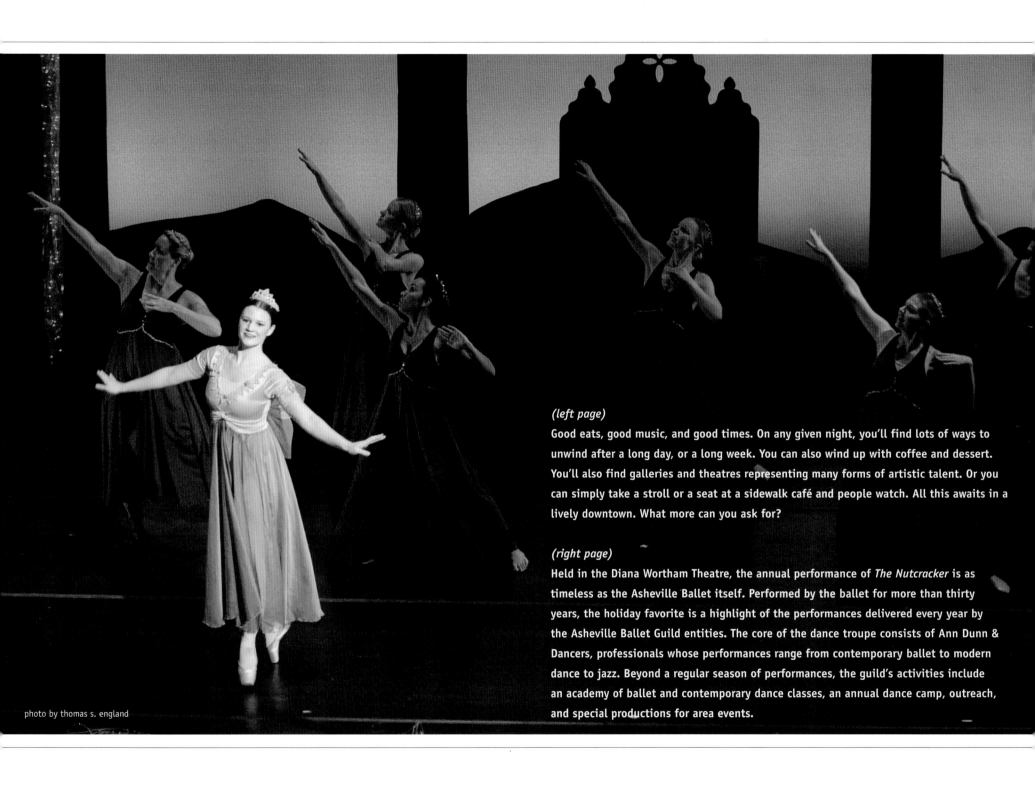

photo by thomas s. england

(left page)

Good eats, good music, and good times. On any given night, you'll find lots of ways to unwind after a long day, or a long week. You can also wind up with coffee and dessert. You'll also find galleries and theatres representing many forms of artistic talent. Or you can simply take a stroll or a seat at a sidewalk café and people watch. All this awaits in a lively downtown. What more can you ask for?

(right page)

Held in the Diana Wortham Theatre, the annual performance of *The Nutcracker* is as timeless as the Asheville Ballet itself. Performed by the ballet for more than thirty years, the holiday favorite is a highlight of the performances delivered every year by the Asheville Ballet Guild entities. The core of the dance troupe consists of Ann Dunn & Dancers, professionals whose performances range from contemporary ballet to modern dance to jazz. Beyond a regular season of performances, the guild's activities include an academy of ballet and contemporary dance classes, an annual dance camp, outreach, and special productions for area events.

It's no wonder that the Blue Ridge Parkway is considered America's Favorite Drive. A cruise along the parkway just north of Asheville takes motorists like Peter McGuire and Robyn Bacon away from the hustle and bustle of the city and into some of the most beautiful terrain in the Carolinas. From mountain views to meadow vistas, the scenes one sees from this amazing roadway are like postcards come to life. And because parking is typically permitted along the road shoulders, it's easy to stop the car at any time and take a few moments to delight in the breathtaking surroundings.

photo by scott indermaur

foreword

On behalf of the Asheville Area Chamber of Commerce Board of Directors and the Chamber staff, I am delighted to present this photographic portrait of the Asheville area.

Asheville is a diverse and unique city that offers residents some of the finest art, theatre, and music in the South. The area's rivers and mountains make this one of the premier outdoor destinations in the world. Our small businesses, and manufacturing, tourism, medical, and service industries provide jobs to more than four hundred thousand residents and their families.

From its very beginning as a convergence of two Cherokee footpaths, Asheville has been a crossroads. That spirit remains strong today as Asheville is a city with local opportunities and global possibilities. The products created in the Asheville area are used worldwide and improve safety, productivity, and quality of life. Our area's natural beauty, high standard of living, and quality workforce continue to draw industry, entrepreneurs, and visitors.

This book paints a portrait of Asheville's charm and beauty and captures her spirit, embodied in creative solutions and a strategic vision designed to enhance the region's economic vitality while protecting our exceptional quality of life.

Through the arts, retail and health-care establishments, and outdoor recreation, Asheville has earned a reputation as one of the most beautiful cities in which to live and work, and a top vacation destination for millions of visitors worldwide. Excite in the adventure of whitewater rafting, enjoy a scenic drive on the Blue Ridge Parkway, visit our many crafts and antique shops, and get to know some of us who are proud to call Asheville home. We invite you to explore Asheville.

Richard J. Lutovsky
President and CEO, Asheville Area Chamber of Commerce

ASHEVILLE
a photographic portrait

would not have been possible without the support of the following sponsors:

Asheville Cabins of Willow Winds • Asheville Vein Center & Medical Spa • Beverly-Hanks & Associates • BH Commercial • Biltmore Farms Commercial • Biltmore Farms Communities • Biltmore Farms Homes • Biltmore Farms Hotel Doubletree • Biltmore Farms, LLC • Carolina Day School • Carolina First Bank • Dixon Hughes PLLC • George W. Morosani & Associates • Groce Funeral Home • Kimmel & Associates • Mission Health & Hospitals • Mountain Air Country Club • Plasticard Locktech International • Preferred Properties of Asheville • Pulliam Properties Inc. • Timothy E. Gillespie, DMD, FAGD

Asheville Vein Center & Medical Spa

Laura B. Ellis, MD • Allan D. Huffman, MD, FACS

Beverly -Hanks & ASSOCIATES

BH Commercial
A Division of Beverly-Hanks & Associates

BILTMORE FARMS ℠
COMMERCIAL

BILTMORE FARMS ℠
COMMUNITIES

BILTMORE FARMS ℠
HOMES

DOUBLETREE®
BILTMORE HOTEL
ASHEVILLE

A Biltmore Farms Hotel

BILTMORE FARMS ℠
Established 1897

CAROLINA
DAY SCHOOL

CAROLINA FIRST
We take your banking personally.

DIXON HUGHES PLLC
Certified Public Accountants and Advisors

GEORGE W.
MOROSANI
& ASSOCIATES

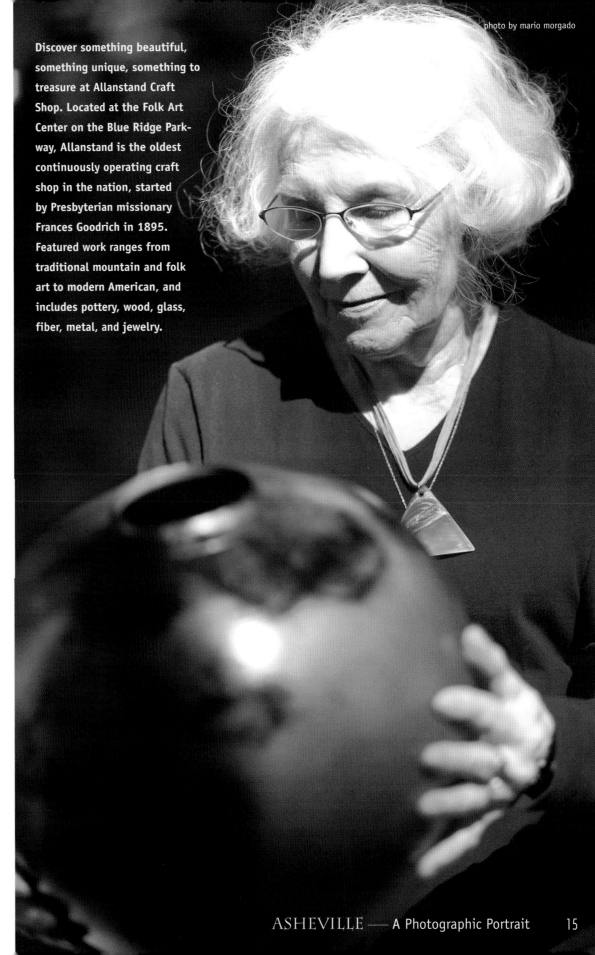

photo by mario morgado

Discover something beautiful, something unique, something to treasure at Allanstand Craft Shop. Located at the Folk Art Center on the Blue Ridge Parkway, Allanstand is the oldest continuously operating craft shop in the nation, started by Presbyterian missionary Frances Goodrich in 1895. Featured work ranges from traditional mountain and folk art to modern American, and includes pottery, wood, glass, fiber, metal, and jewelry.

Obtained by the town in 1936 for use as a community recreational center, Lake Louise is one of Weaverville's most treasured public gathering places. Located at the intersection of Merrimon Avenue and Lakeshore Drive, its facilities include picnic areas, barbecue grills, playground equipment, a workout center, a half-mile walking trail, and restrooms. Fishing is allowed from the shoreline with a purchase of a permit. Each May Lake Louise is also the site for Weaverville's Arbor Day Celebration, during which dozens of volunteers turn out to plant trees and enjoy a day of springtime fun. Such is Weaverville's pride in its natural environment that each year since 1990 the National Arbor Day Foundation has named it as a Tree City USA in recognition of its urban forestry program.

photo by rod reilly

Exhilaration in its purest form. Whether sliding down rocks or maneuvering a

photo by scott indermaur

river's twists and turns, nothing beats the excitement of a run through the rapids.

photo by rod reilly

ASHEVILLE —— **A Photographic Portrait**

photo by rod reilly

water ways

(far left)

Many hikers in the Asheville area cite Dupont State Forest near Brevard as one of their favorite waterfall treks. Located about forty miles southwest of Asheville, this ten-thousand-acre North Carolina state forest has nine hundred miles of hiking trails punctuated with stunning waterfalls and plenty of places to stop, cool your feet, and have a picnic.

(left)

The Graveyard Fields Loop off the Blue Ridge Parkway in Pisgah National Forest also features some stunning waterfalls. The trail is approximately three and a half miles long and takes about two hours. Hikers and dogs agree that it's one of the most popular in the forest.

photo by thomas s. england

Asheville's temperate climate makes it a place of year-round comfort. With average daily temperatures ranging from thirty-seven degrees in January to seventy-three degrees in July, and humidity hovering around 58 percent, spending time outdoors is one of the great pleasures of living here. The city rests on a plateau and is surrounded by mountain ranges, some exceeding five thousand feet in elevation, which provide a natural backdrop for four distinctive, changing seasons.

GIVING AND SHARING: watchwords at kimmel & associates inc.

photo by rod reilly

▲ Kimmel & Associates sponsors a health program that includes running events, a softball team, and yoga classes. Employees Hardy Ward, Michael Murphy, Ben Schlaefer, and Dennis Myers are getting a workout jogging down Page Avenue.

The scorched, water-stained five-dollar bill hangs proudly in the office of Joe Kimmel, owner and president of Kimmel & Associates Inc., as a talisman from a bygone era when that bill represented a significant portion of his personal wealth. Now the head of a 150-person company, Kimmel remembers that earlier time with a fondness for the principles it taught him: grace, faith, and generosity. Evidence of those virtues acting in Kimmel's life abound; his company recently gave $6.92 million to Western Carolina University to establish the Kimmel School of Construction Management, Engineering and Technology; he also gave $2 million to the Center for Health and Wellness complex at the University of North Carolina, Asheville (UNCA).

"I was given that five dollars to start my new life the day I got out of prison," said Kimmel with a hint of laughter in his voice. Not that the story is a joke: it isn't. "The IRS sent me to jail for a year because I failed to file a tax return." Obviously, there is more to his story.

"I was the first person in my family to go to college, and although I was vitally interested in art, writing, and poetry, I decided to pick the hardest major I could find, and that was nuclear engineering. My idea was to make some money and then go back to art, which was what I loved. And I did. I made—

(continued on page 26)

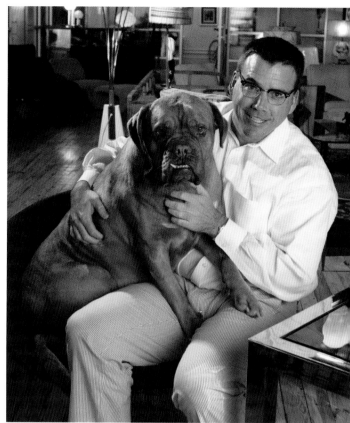

Joe Kimmel, owner of Kimmel & Associates Inc., and his son Charlie, chief operating officer, share the company's credo of giving and sharing. The official philosophy states, "It is our mission to assist in the corporate growth of our clients; to assist in the personal growth of our candidates; to grow profitably; and to honor God in all we do."

photo by rod reilly

photo by rod reilly

"It is our mission to assist in the corporate growth of our clients; to assist in the personal growth of our candidates; to grow profitably; and to honor God in all we do."

Not many people—outside of museum employees—actually get to work in the midst of an art collection. However, employees of Kimmel & Associates can enjoy owner Joe Kimmel's interest in the art deco era every day as they walk through the company's common areas. The official Kimmel Collection, Art That Works: A Celebration of Design, was donated to the Fine Art Museum at Western Carolina University. It represents thirty years of loving acquisitions.

(Kimmel & Associates continued from page 25)

and lost—a lot of money, and that's when I ran into trouble with the IRS. But being in prison was a wonderful experience. I came to the end of myself and found out about grace and God and the incredible power of giving and serving. It's the basis of our business now."

Kimmel's credo of giving and sharing is evident in the company philosophy, which states, "It is our mission to assist in the corporate growth of our clients; to assist in the personal growth of our candidates; to grow profitably; and to honor God in all we do."

"Joe always says, 'Work with a servant's heart, and the benefits will come back multiplied,'" explains Paul Samuels, executive vice president. "In practice, it works like this: there are two sides to our business, clients and candidates. Our clients are the companies who choose us to find the best possible candidates to lead divisions or projects, while the candidates themselves are the professionals looking to make strategic career moves and trust us to be their mentors. We treat both groups with respect and address their needs with urgency.

"There is actually a third important component, and that is the dedication of the employees here at Kimmel. Joe is a phenomenal leader; this is a difficult job, and he inspires and encourages all of us."

Kimmel & Associates, which has been in Asheville more than twenty-five years, is the largest executive search firm in the nation specializing in the construction industry. Working with a staff of professional recruiters and consultants, the company places an average of thirteen hundred candidates with top companies annually.

Training at Kimmel is serious business. The company conducts a fifty-session certification program in which experienced consultants pass on their accumulated knowledge to new recruiters.

Kimmel's emphasis on learning does not stop there. Since 2004, Kimmel & Associates has awarded the Scholarship for Students in Construction to more than 180 students at colleges and universities in thirty-four states. In addition, Kimmel funds the Joe W. Kimmel Scholarship for First Generation Students of Promise at UNCA, where six of his seven children attended school. The scholarship helps first-generation students who "don't necessarily have the flashiest grade-point average, but whose work and efforts show great promise."

Obviously, Joe Kimmel has met his initial goal "to make some money." But what about his love of art? The answer to that question is evident in the donation of the Kimmel Collection, Art That Works: A Celebration of Design, to the new Fine Art Museum at Western Carolina University. This diverse collection is the culmination of thirty years of loving acquisitions.

Kimmel has even come full circle back to his desire to be an artist. He is the conceptual creator of a line of jewelry, including pendants and accessories made from twenty-three-karat pure gold, a pursuit that reflects his interest in the art deco era.

All in all, Joe Kimmel's philosophy of giving and sharing has been a blessing to him, to his family, to his associates, and to the Asheville community. ❖

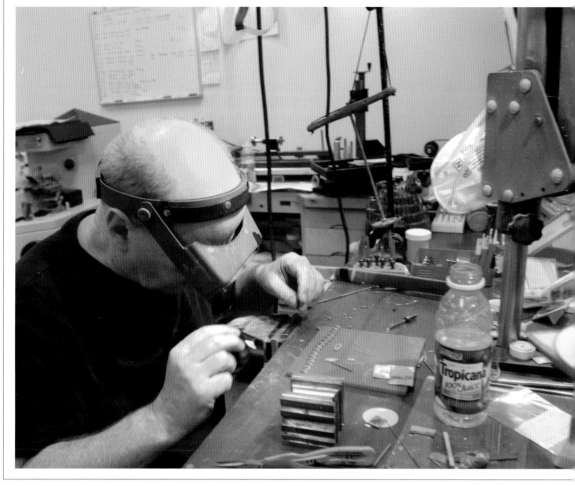

photo by rod reilly

Kimmel & Associates is the largest executive search firm in the nation specializing in the construction industry. The founder, Joe Kimmel, has always been interested in art. "My idea after I graduated from college was to make some money and then go back to art." He has done both. Today he is the conceptual creator of a line of jewelry made from twenty-three-karat pure gold. His concepts are executed by Kenneth Cope, master jeweler at J. Kimmel Fine Jewelry.

photo by kristalyn bunyan

(left page)
Morning music classics, afternoon workshops, and after-dinner demonstrations and concerts on the lawn . . . participants in Old Time Music Week can choose classes in the specialties of instrumental music, singing, storytelling, or dance. Enroll or simply stroll; it's all about the country arts of entertainment and a tradition worthy of preservation.

(right page)
Sponsored by Mars Hill College in Mars Hill, North Carolina, the Blue Ridge Old Time Music Week promises days full of fun and learning. No experience is necessary, just a common interest in the historical music of Appalachia and a yen to take a class or join a front-porch jam session with a friend.

photo by kristalyn bunyan

DR. TIMOTHY E. GILLESPIE: thriving practice, active lifestyle

photo by rod reilly

▲ Even staff meetings are fun at Dr. Gillespie's Cosmetic, Implant & General Dentistry practice, where members of the team round out discussions with activities like a little creative candle-making. The energetic, yet warm and caring environment of the practice translates to a feeling of comfort for patients.

Asheville offers a unique style of living that is especially attractive to professionals like Timothy E. Gillespie, DMD, FAGD, who enjoys being able to balance a thriving dental practice with both recreational and cultural opportunities.

After a stint as a research chemist, Dr. Gillespie turned to dentistry and, upon graduation, opened a private practice in Asheville in 1993. That practice has grown to encompass a comprehensive scope of services, from dental checkups and cleanings to cosmetic enhancements and restorative treatments to periodontal disease management and implants for missing teeth.

Helping Dr. Gillespie provide the latest advances in dentistry are an associate dentist and a dozen personnel, some of whom have been with the practice from the start. Their loyalty stems, in part, from an office culture that makes going to work a pleasure. "Our office culture is a high-energy environment, but it's also a very warm, family-type environment," says Dr. Gillespie, adding that everyone comes together for periodic special outings outside office hours as well. "We have a lot of fun together, and it really fosters cohesion among our staff."

(continued on page 32)

Bicycling on the Blue Ridge Parkway is one of the many outdoor activities Dr. Gillespie enjoys in his spare time, alone or with family and friends. Asheville's natural beauty beckons residents to enjoy time in the great outdoors.

photo by mario morgado

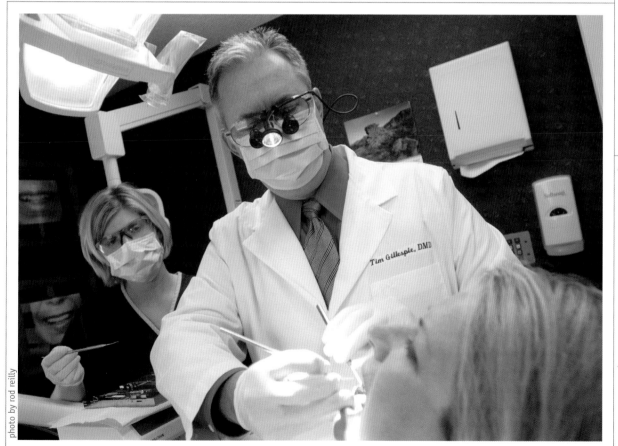

photo by rod reilly

Dr. Gillespie and team offer a comprehensive scope of services for patients, from routine dental procedures to the latest advances in cosmetic enhancements, restorative treatments, periodontal disease management, and implants for missing teeth.

"Our office culture is a high-energy environment, but it's also a very warm, family-type environment."

(Dr. Timothy E. Gillespie, continued from page 31)

Patients take comfort in that feeling of unity and in an atmosphere geared toward calming concerns. In addition to taking a real interest in each patient's personal well-being, Dr. Gillespie and staff use education as a means of dispelling anxiety about procedures that some patients consider intimidating. "The more patients know about procedures themselves, the less fearful they become," says Dr. Gillespie. "They have more control over the process, and then they can educate others by telling them how a certain procedure went for them and how happy they are with the results."

Education is also vital to Dr. Gillespie's ongoing interest in his profession. "It's my intense desire to be a continuous learner," he says. "Dentistry is not a static profession; it's very exciting. We're constantly doing research, identifying new materials to use, and finding better ways of doing things, and I like to keep myself apprised of the new advances and techniques."

But being able to enjoy a stimulating profession is only one part of what life is about in Asheville. A devoted family man, celebrating twenty years of marriage and actively involved in the activities of three growing sons, Dr. Gillespie takes advantage of Asheville's cultural and recreational opportunities too.

In addition to family activities, and regular musical performances as a trumpet player in his church's brass ensemble, Gillespie is an avid outdoorsman, particularly drawn to hiking, camping, fishing, and bicycling. "In Asheville, we're very fortunate to have such natural beauty that it really drives you outdoors anyway," he says. "But I love being able to tend to the physical aspect of my life in addition to the professional aspect. It's all about balance, really—being able to enjoy an overall balance of life."

That symmetry also allows Dr. Gillespie a firm foundation for giving time and talent in service to others at home and abroad. From local clinics for kids to mission trips south of the border, Dr. Gillespie knows the importance of helping others enjoy a better quality of life. "I'm from a small town, and so it's part of that feeling of community that I grew up with," he says. "I've been given a lot, and it's extremely important to me to acknowledge that and appreciate that by giving back." ❖

photo by mario morgado

▲ Dr. Gillespie in the sanctuary of First Baptist Church, Asheville, where he is a member of the Brass Ensemble. In addition to a thriving dental practice, Dr. Gillespie enjoys participation in some of the many cultural activities that Asheville has to offer.

A

As perfect as a painting, this tranquil setting invites visitors to cross over the bridge and spend a few minutes in quiet meditation basking in the sun and listening to the sounds of nature.

photo by scott indermaur

photo by rod reilly

photo by alan s. weiner

(far left)

On a cool, misty morning in Asheville, David Olson *(left)* and Irby Brinson *(right)* pull on their waders and take to the pristine waters of the French Broad River for some fly-fishing. The renowned river, which runs through the picturesque setting of the Blue Ridge Mountains, is known for its excellent wild and native trout fishing. For experienced anglers like Olson and Brinson, the year-round fly-fishing opportunities in this part of North Carolina are too good to be missed. And even for those new to the sport, there are numerous fly-fishing schools in the area that will have novices casting—and catching like pros in no time.

(left and above)

The freedom of the open road and the ability to enjoy nature's surroundings while also getting a good workout are elements of what draws bicycling enthusiasts to the sport. Given the region's numerous trails, that workout can be as relaxing or as challenging as you want. If you're just getting started, give the Blue Ridge Bicycle Club a call. Established in 1974 as a road cycling club, the increased interest in mountain biking led to the beginning of trail maintenance programs in cooperation with the U.S. Forest Service. Today the BRBC has around 250 members who participate in organized road and trail rides year-round.

photo by mario morgado

photo by scott indermaur

(far left)
Forget the big-box stores or the harried malls. Instead, take a leisurely stroll along downtown Asheville's friendly streets and sneak a peek through the display windows or dart in and out of the myriad galleries and shops as the mood strikes you.

(left)
Since 1982, Malaprop's Bookstore/Café has been a place where local and visiting bibliophiles feel right at home. Voted *Publishers Weekly* Bookseller of the Year in 2000, Malaprop's is a locally owned, independent bookstore that also serves coffee, beverages, and sweet and savory menu items. David and Andrea Steney, of McClellanville, South Carolina, made use of the free wireless connection while in downtown Asheville, where the shop is located. In addition to the latest releases, Malaprop's sells used and out-of-print books through its Downtown Books and News shop. Malaprop's promotes reading through author readings, monthly book clubs, and other community activities.

(this page)
Western North Carolina has attracted retirees for many years now. Most are everyday folk who are drawn by the area's quality of life. Others are people whose work we've enjoyed, like poet Carl Sandburg, who moved here at the age of sixty-seven. Yet Sandburg didn't really retire. He spent the remaining twenty-two years of his life in this home in Flat Rock, living out a sentiment he once stated: "Retirement is okay, as long as it doesn't interfere with your work."

photo by scott indermaur

EXPLORE ASHEVILLE at the Chamber's one-stop shop

photo by scott indermaur

▲ If you want to know what's happenin', check out the activities board at the Asheville Visitor Center. It provides twenty-four-hour information including maps, weather forecasts, area attractions, live music performances, theatre, festivals, and almost always, a surprise or two.

"Good morning, may I help you?"
"Yes, I need some information about vacationing in Asheville."
"I can help you with that."
"And I might want to relocate my business. Who handles that?"
"I can help you with that too."
"What if I want to check out the real estate market? Where do I go for that?"
"You can get all that information right here. Our president likes to say the Asheville Area Chamber of Commerce is a one-stop shop. And we're right downtown."
"Downtown? I'll never find a parking space!"
"Actually, we have 150 spaces right at our front door."
"Terrific. I like this city already."
"Yes, sir, that's the way we planned it."

▲ Richard J. Lutovsky, president and CEO, Asheville Area Chamber of Commerce.

photo by scott indermaur

This typical phone conversation points out the fact that, unlike most chambers, the Asheville Area Chamber of Commerce also houses the Asheville Convention & Visitors Bureau and the Economic Development Coalition of Asheville–Buncombe County. All are located in the Chamber's convenient new building, which nearly tripled the previous space.

"We're one of the largest Chambers in the Southeast," said president Richard J. Lutovsky. "We support what we call the four-legged Asheville economic stool. That includes tourism, small business, health care, and diverse manufacturing."

Apparently, the formula is working, because Asheville consistently receives top marks in a wide range of categories.

For example, *American Style* ranks Asheville number-two of the Top 25 Small Town Arts Destinations. *Forbes* lists it in the top twenty-five Large Metros Best Places for Business and Careers. *National Geographic's Adventure* magazine touts Asheville as One of Ten Great Adventure Towns, and one of four cities recommended for mountain biking. *Parents* magazine calls it a Top Family Getaway; *USA Today* says it is one of Five Cities That Are Special; and *Self* magazine calls it America's Happiest City for Women. Most recently, Asheville was named one of Frommer's top-twelve travel destinations for 2007.

"Another unique feature of this Chamber," said Lutovsky, "is that each year we take fifty-five of our citizens to other cities like Providence, Rhode Island; Austin, Texas; or Portland, Oregon, to study their best ideas and put them to work here."

Another important facet of the Chamber is the Economic Development Coalition (EDC), which works for both Asheville and Buncombe County. Asheville has record-setting job levels and unemployment well below the national average. Couple that with balanced economic growth, an emerging professional services sector, and the transformation of the manufacturing sector, and the city is poised—as the EDC mission states—"to attract and expand business opportunities while improving the well-being of our citizens."

The tourism community's new slogan, "Asheville Any Way You Like It," seems appropriate for a city with such a healthy balance between art, lifestyle, and business opportunities. ❖

Asheville has record-setting job levels and unemployment well below the national average.

education for a lifetime

Dedicated to fostering personal and academic excellence, educational institutions throughout the Asheville region support diversity, community, and personal development both inside and outside the classroom. Whether participating in a decorative restoration project, assisting in the school's nursery, or meeting with fellow students to organize a campus initiative, students develop a strong sense of purpose, place, and participation that they will carry throughout their lives. Choices for higher education abound. Warren Wilson College, an independent, accredited, four-year liberal arts college, awards bachelor's of arts and bachelor's of science degrees in a variety of disciplines as well as a master's of fine arts degree in creative writing. The University of North Carolina at Asheville, a public four-year liberal arts college, provides the kind of education that changes lives and inspires others to do the same. A highly valued community resource, the Asheville-Buncombe Technical Community College provides excellent academic and continuing education opportunities for nearly twenty-five thousand students in Western North Carolina.

SISTERS OF MERCY SERVICES CORPORATION — evolving with asheville

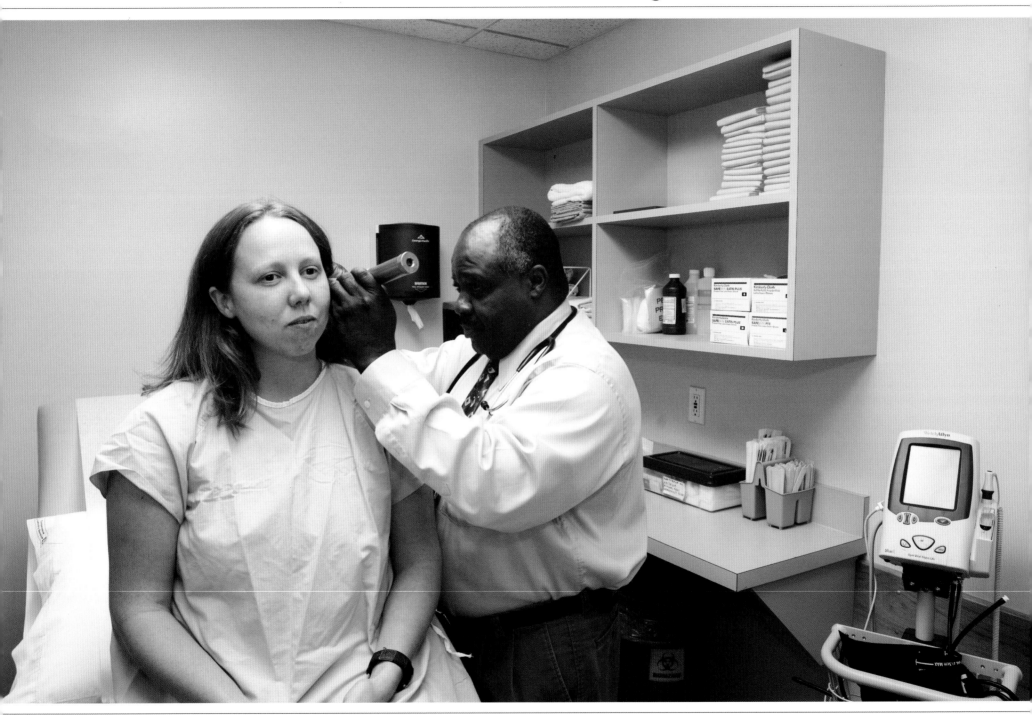

photo by alan s. weiner

▲ Caring, board-certified physicians minister to patients at
Sisters of Mercy Urgent Care.

Asheville looks very different from the way it did more than a century ago, having changed and developed as the population grew. The same thing can be said about Sisters of Mercy, an organization that has dedicated itself to serving the health-care needs of the local community since 1900. Then, the Sisters of Mercy in Western North Carolina operated an eighteen-bed tuberculosis sanatorium in Asheville. Today, as Sisters of Mercy Services Corporation, it offers a broad spectrum of health-care services, ranging from urgent care to behavioral health.

"I think it's unique that the sponsoring agency of our ministries has had such an enduring presence here in Asheville," says Sister Maria Goretti, director of mission and values for Sisters of Mercy. "We came in response to the needs of the time then, and we have adapted and adjusted to respond to the needs of the time of the people that we serve."

With three dedicated facilities in Asheville, Sisters of Mercy Urgent Care is a key component for the organization. Offering affordable, quality medical care, Urgent Care ensures that every man, woman, and child who walks through the door has access to outstanding health-care resources provided by board-certified physicians and licensed clinical staff. In addition, according to executive director Shana Duncan, Sisters of Mercy Urgent Care features the Compassionate Care Program, a tiered discount process that provides financial assistance to those who need it most.

Sisters of Mercy Services also includes ARP/Phoenix, a comprehensive substance abuse assessment, treatment, and prevention services provider. Focusing on patient-centered care, ARP/Phoenix helps individuals and families through two adult and youth outpatient facilities and two twenty-four-hour residential treatment facilities: the Mary Benson House and the Neil Dobbins Center. "As with Urgent Care," explains executive director Paul Tax, "we operate under the core values of Sacredness of Life, Human Dignity, Mercy, Justice, Service, and Excellence."

Those six values are the driving force behind the entire Sisters of Mercy Services family of companies—from Health Designs, the occupational health division that provides onsite health care to business, industries, and schools; to the for-profit Mountain Health Contracting, in operation for twenty-two years, providing general contracting services to physicians and other health-care providers, as well as building two affordable homes; and the nonprofit McAuley Foundation that supports the mission and ministry of the Sisters of Mercy of Western North Carolina. And while Sisters of Mercy Services is unwavering in its adherence to those values, it continues to search for new ways to benefit the community, which includes a recent emphasis on striving to boost residents' overall health by placing a spotlight on prevention and wellness.

"We are working collaboratively with other community organizations to promote wellness," notes Tim Johnston, Sisters of Mercy Services' president and CEO. Adds Duncan, "All of our companies are heading in the same direction, with a common set of goals, which are to provide our services and meet the needs of the people we serve as we follow the core values of the Sisters of Mercy." ❖

ARP/Phoenix's licensed counselors assist individuals and families by providing substance abuse and behavioral health counseling and treatment services in a confidential, professional, and person-centered approach.

photo by alan s. weiner

"We operate under the core values of Sacredness of Life, Human Dignity, Mercy, Justice, Service, and Excellence."

ASHEVILLE —— A Photographic Portrait   43

photo by tim barnwell

photo by tim barnwell

BH COMMERCIAL: real estate for business

photo by rod reilly

BH Commercial's team of consummate professionals is ready to provide prompt, positive results. By combining their knowledge and passion for success, the BH Commercial team is able to give clients the million-dollar treatment they deserve.

ounded in 1976, Beverly-Hanks & Associates, Realtors has grown to become the largest full-service commercial brokerage firm in Western North Carolina. In 2006, BH Commercial developed its own identity within the family of Beverly-Hanks brands. Their roots here are deep within this community, and the team's members have developed solid, long-term relationships with clients. Knowledgeable, experienced, customer-focused brokers are committed to providing results for their customers that exceed expectations.

Since the hallmark of this organization is its ability to attract and retain quality associates who provide service that is second to none, the team comprises a broad range of consummate professionals: experienced Brokers and a dedicated support staff who are committed to providing prompt, positive results. No one knows the commercial market better. Knowledge coupled with passion and enhanced by experience has allowed BH Commercial to serve clients and broker transactions of all types and sizes, with all receiving the million-dollar treatment they deserve.

BH Commercial offers a broad spectrum of professional services designed to effectively match the needs of its customers. A full-service brokerage firm, BH Commercial offers sales and marketing services for industrial, warehouse, multifamily, retail, and office properties; land acquisition; leasing administration; and real estate investment consultation. The BH Commercial Team also represents buyers and tenants in the search for appropriate commercial properties.

Through its affiliations with the Society of Industrial and Office Realtors (SIOR), Certified Commercial Investment Member (CCIM), and the International Council of Shopping Centers (ICSC), BH Commercial connects worldwide. ❖

BH Commercial looks at the present and into the future when working with clients, helping to prepare for today's successes and growth for tomorrow.

photo by rod reilly

The team comprises a broad range of consummate professionals: experienced Brokers and a dedicated support staff who are committed to providing prompt, positive results.

photo by alan s. weiner

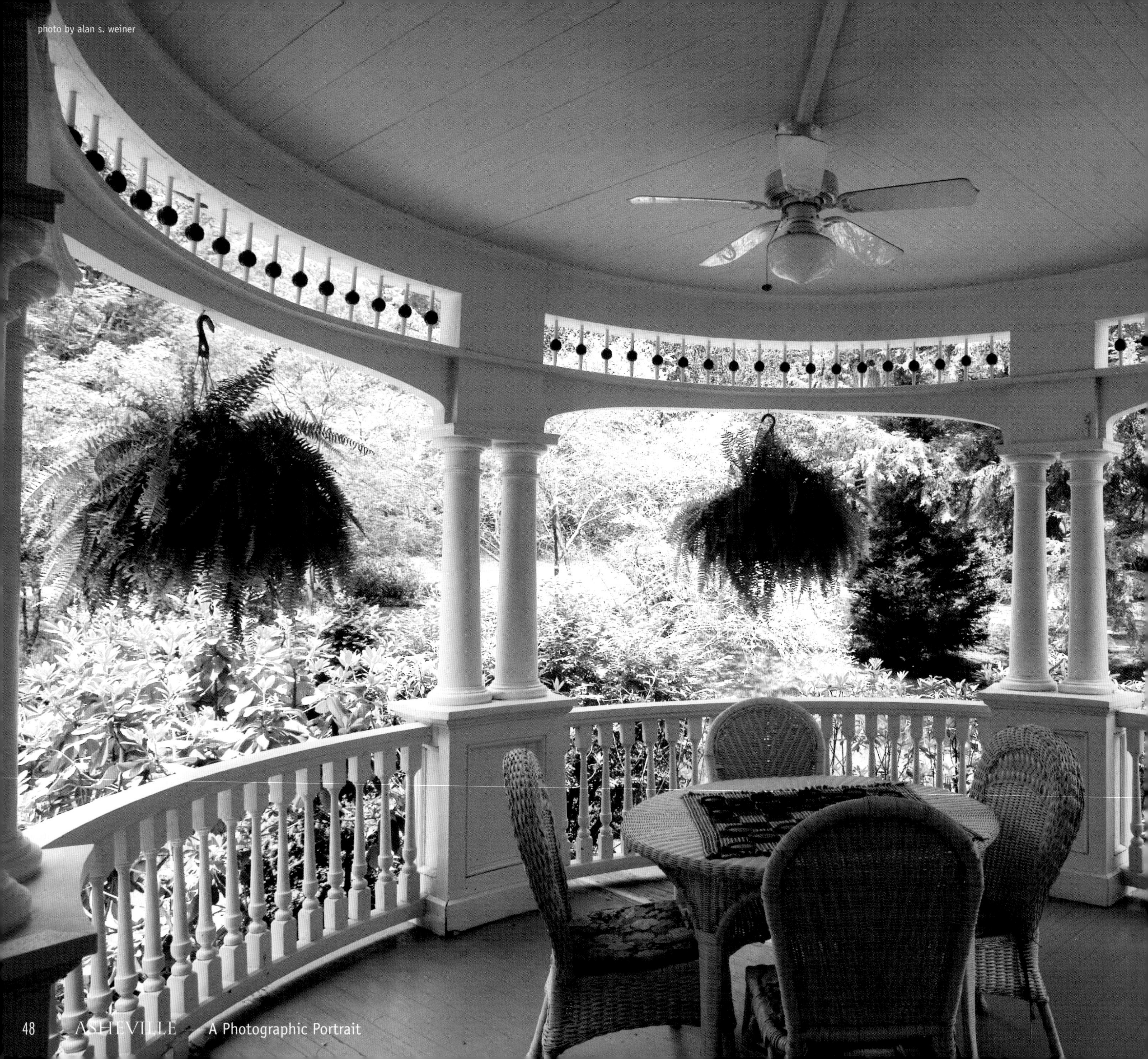

photo by alan s. weiner

A Legacy of Hospitality

The bed-and-breakfast concept has been around since human beings first started going from one place to another. Early on, monasteries served the overnight needs of travelers. Later B&Bs became popular in Europe. As the trend spread, they went by many names, such as paradors, pensions, *gasthaus*, *minskukus*, *shukukos*, and *pousados*, depending on their country of origin. Here in the United States, pioneers often sought refuge in homes, inns, and taverns. Some of these historic accommodations still offer comfort to the weary traveler. Guests who prefer a homey atmosphere will find a wide range of choices in the Asheville area, including the Princess Ann Hotel, Richmond Hill Inn, and the 1900 Inn on Monford. Innkeepers like Jim and Linda Palmer (left), who run the The Lion and the Rose Bed and Breakfast, offer guests not only southern hospitality, but also modern amenities. It is well worth the time to check out all that Asheville has to offer in the way of charm, service, attention to details, and, of course, a sumptuous breakfast.

photo by mario morgado

W

hat greater comfort can be given a traveler

photo by rod reilly

photo by alan s. weiner

photo by mario morgado

photo by alan s. weiner

B & B WRIGHT INN & CARRIAGE HOUSE

than the promise of an open door and a warm heart?

McGUIRE, WOOD & BISSETTE, P.A. — where client service is key

photo by mario morgado

▲ Located in vibrant downtown Asheville, McGuire, Wood & Bissette, P.A., serves clients throughout Western North Carolina and across the region and nation—representing individuals, small businesses, and large corporations by protecting their interests in all areas of the law.

For more than a century, the law firm of McGuire, Wood & Bissette, P.A., has provided a wealth of expertise and quality legal work for business, industry, and families throughout Western North Carolina. The core of the firm's philosophy is a set of shared values that influence how each client matter is handled: with integrity, honesty, and enjoyment of the work at hand.

"Our collective goal has always been to provide our clients with excellent service," explains president Louis Bissette. That mission is the foundation upon which the firm was founded in 1894, when Asheville native Haywood Parker gave up teaching to become a lawyer. Throughout the subsequent decades, as the firm grew and evolved to include the practice areas of business, corporations and securities, health care, litigation, estate planning, and real estate, among many others, the desire to protect clients' interests was unwavering. Today, McGuire, Wood & Bissette, P.A., remains committed to upholding that tradition and continues to find unique ways to help its clients not only get results, but also feel supported through the legal process.

The firm draws upon the diverse skills and experiences of its attorneys, many of whom are board-certified in various areas of practice and licensed in several states, including North Carolina, Virginia, Tennessee, Alabama, Georgia, and Illinois. In addition to core legal services, the attorneys at McGuire,

Wood & Bissette, P.A., also share their knowledge and expertise through a number of informational legal-issue seminars such as Estate and Charitable Planning, Avoiding Employment Discrimination, and Construction: Contracts and Lien Law.

McGuire, Wood & Bissette, P.A., is also well-known in Asheville for restoring the historic Drhumor Building, the city's oldest standing commercial building. Constructed circa 1895 in the style of the Romanesque Revival, the Drhumor Building pays tribute to Asheville's fascinating history and architecture. It's a fitting location for the firm, which has had an enduring presence in Asheville thanks to the abiding public service efforts of its members. Several partners have served the city through public office, including attorneys Richard A. Wood Jr. and W. Louis Bissette Jr., each of whom has served as mayor of Asheville. The collective role the attorneys and staff play as involved citizens informs the direction of their legal work, strengthening the firm's offering as a whole to the community.

"We want our attorneys and staff to be involved in volunteer and civic efforts so that we collectively learn more about the community we live in," notes Bissette. "We've been here for more than one hundred years, and it's important to us to work to make this community the best it can be."

From working with clients to serving the community, that dedication is steadfast. At McGuire, Wood & Bissette, P.A., that's the way it's always been—and the way it always will be. ❖

▲ McGuire, Wood & Bissette, P.A., draws upon the diverse skills and experiences of its twenty-plus attorneys. Knowledgeable, accessible, and with enjoyment of the work at hand, the firm's attorneys have a special connection to the neighbors they serve.

photo by mario morgado

"Our collective goal has always been to provide our clients with excellent service," explains president Louis Bissette.

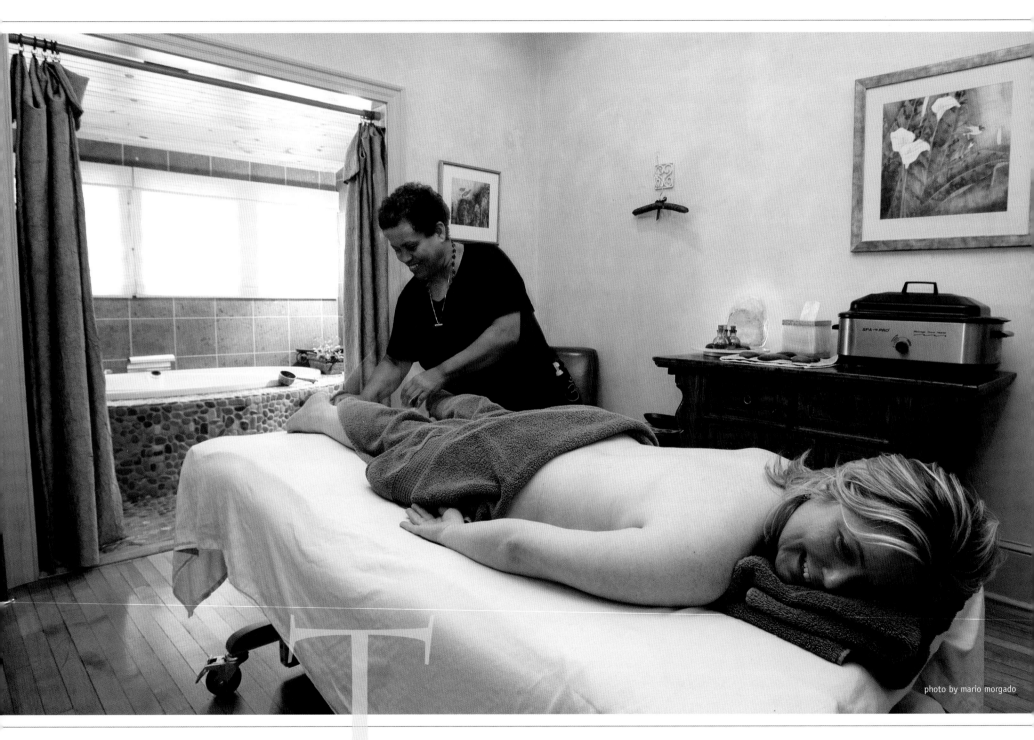

his is relaxation at its finest. Pampering galore, and a

photo by alan s. weiner

photo by mario morgado

photo by mario morgado

relax Asheville's centuries-old reputation as a center for mental, physical, and spiritual rejuvenation is alive and well. Whether high up in the mountain or in the heart of the city, dozens of resorts and day spas provide the weary visitor with invigorating and restorative treatments. Pop in for a hot and cold soak or expert massage, or make time for a lengthier respite of holistic treatments and lifestyle education classes.

heavenly place to rejuvenate the mind, body, and spirit.

THE *ASHEVILLE CITIZEN-TIMES*: reaching readers anytime, anywhere

▲ Nanci Bompey, *Asheville Citizen-Times* health and environment reporter, gathers reader comments for the newspaper's local information center.

photo by bill sanders

Why wait to get today's news tomorrow? Today's *Asheville Citizen-Times* is using the latest technology to streamline consumer access to news, around the clock.

The *Asheville Citizen-Times* is mirroring the newspaper industry's transition as it develops new products across diverse media channels to reach consumers anytime, anywhere. Always the community watchdog, the *Citizen-Times* is now leveraging its greatest strength: local news.

"Our readers want to be engaged and influenced, and to feel connected with the Western North Carolina experience. They want to know that the newspaper was written with them in mind," says executive editor Susan Ihne. "Our goal is to give our readers a reason to come to us, every day."

The modern newsroom enables the readers to interact with journalists in real time. Today's *Asheville Citizen-Times* newsroom now contains multimedia journalists who provide the fastest and deepest coverage of stories and issues in print and online. The result of this evolution is more local news content in print and online, and more news submitted by the local community and beyond. The print product showcases this approach with new and consolidated sections, new features, and expanded local content—the most notable being the "hyper-local" reader-submitted news about local people, communities, schools, and more.

The online channel, Citizen-Times.com, is the most visited Web site in Western North Carolina, averaging more than 5 million page views a month. To serve readers better, the site now offers a powerful local search engine on every Web page, allowing the user to find everything from recent news articles and events to local restaurants and retailers.

"In short, the *Citizen-Times* is becoming a premier provider of digital and print information, and a hub of community interaction through technology," says Jeffrey Green, president and publisher. ❖

"Our readers want to be engaged and influenced, and to feel connected with the Western North Carolina experience."

For Wink and her owner, Christine Gait, a stop at Three Dog Bakery is a must after their walk. "Wink loves to stop by for a drink of water and a treat," she says. "And everyone knows her by name." Owner Tom Flora, who opened the shop in August 2006, says the great thing about running the bakery is that "everyone involved—employees, customers, and the dogs—has such a good time in here." Even Flora's own pooches get in on the act: his two wire-haired Dachshunds spend enough time in the shop to warrant customized business cards.

A stay at the Grove Park Inn Resort and Spa is like stepping back into time—only with the world-class service and amenities of the present. The exterior of the main inn remains today much as it did when it was originally built in 1913. That same grand style is reflected in the natural rock used to create the forty-thousand-square-foot spa's underground grottolike pool and waterfalls. Even the golf course is rich in history. Opened for play in 1899, it was redesigned in 1924 by the great Donald Ross.

photo by rod reilly

a haven for the arts

photo by rod reilly

photo by thomas s. england

Maybe it's the quality of light, the abundance of natural beauty, or an appreciative and accepting community, but almost from its founding Asheville has been a locus for the visual arts. Today, Asheville's status as a top marketplace for professional American arts and crafts not only generates over $140 million a year for the region's economy, it also places the city at the top of many national rankings, including America's Top 25 Arts Destinations (*AmericanStyle* 2006) and twenty-fourth among 200 Large Metros Best Places for Business and Careers (*Forbes* 2006). Given Western North Carolina's history of craft-making, many local artisans naturally devote themselves to preserving indigenous forms. Each year the nonprofit North Carolina Quilt Symposium provides visitors up close and personal views of the best of the quilting medium. Modern interpretations are celebrated as well, from the large-scale abstract wall relief sculptures of George Handy to the luminous raku pottery of Steven Forbes deSoule. Still other artisans, like Julie Larson, bring an American sensibility to Old World European porcelain glazing techniques with her and her husband Tyrone's finely crafted porcelain serving pieces. For those who want to expand their knowledge of the arts, the Asheville Art Museum features an extensive library and Teacher Resource Center, as well as school tours, workshops, lectures, films, and travel programs.

photo by rod reilly

From the potter's wheel, the painter's brush, and the quilter's needle is

formed a delightful medley of color and form to delight the senses.

PREFERRED PROPERTIES: personal service, personal results

photo by tim barnwell

▲ With a vibrant arts, music, and nightlife scene, downtown Asheville is the jewel of Western North Carolina. Since 1972, four years after it was established, Preferred Properties has been a part of the downtown landscape.

community as appealing and distinctive as Asheville offers many options among real estate brokers, and choosing the one that fits best is a decision to be made carefully. One brokerage, Preferred Properties of Asheville, stands out as uniquely as our community itself.

Founded in 1968, Preferred Properties is a family-owned company that became a leader in the Asheville real estate market by giving highly personalized attention and service to its clients. "When you call one of our offices, you'll speak with your broker," says Terry Horner, agency co-owner. "We understand the financial and emotional investments our clients make when they decide to buy or sell a home. That's why our commitment is to provide them the expertise, care, and service they deserve.

There are no teams here; your broker will walk you through your purchase or sale from start to finish."

Delivering a customer-focused experience is a natural fit for an agency that often works with a discerning clientele. In 2006, the average Preferred Properties transaction was approximately $442,000, a figure more than 25 percent higher than the closest competitor. "We're a full-service agency that works with buyers and sellers across all price ranges, but our knowledge and experience in Asheville's higher-end home market is unmatched," states Jane McNeil, agency co-owner.

Additionally, brokers at Preferred Properties average more than a dozen years of real estate experience and more than $3 million in annual sales. In short, they are experts at bringing together buyers and sellers and are unsurpassed in their efforts to ensure a successful transaction.

(continued on page 66)

photo by tim barnwell

▲ Jane McNeil and Terry Horner are co-owners of Preferred Properties, one of Asheville's finest real estate companies. The firm's reputation stems from a long tradition of being highly attentive to clients' needs and wishes.

◄ Nestled within Asheville, the Biltmore Forest neighborhood is home to some of the area's most elegant addresses.

photo by tim barnwell

One brokerage, Preferred Properties of Asheville, stands out as uniquely as our community itself.

(Preferred Properties continued from page 65)

But, more than the bottom line, brokers at Preferred Properties recognize the importance of quality neighborhoods and a healthy community. That's why the company and its brokers place great importance on giving back to the community. "We know that the success of this community has a direct impact on the success of our company. Without a desirable Asheville, we would not be where we are today," says Horner. From building homes for Habitat for Humanity to serving the hungry through Meals on Wheels to giving hope through contributions to the United Way, Preferred Properties is committed to making a difference in the place it calls home. Horner explains, "There is an inherent sense of responsibility for our community that you'll find in everyone at Preferred Properties."

Preferred Properties' growth has been at a steady pace. The office in downtown Asheville was built in 1972, and a second location in Biltmore Forest was added in 2006. Today thirty-four brokers operate from the two locations. "We are not an agent factory," explains Horner. "Our belief is that quality is better than quantity when it comes to hiring brokers. We are extremely selective in who we ask to join our company; we recognize we're not for everyone. It always comes back to what—and who—is best for our clients. That's why we only hire the best."

Emphasizing professionalism, integrity, a personable attitude, and a strong willingness to go the extra mile for clients has contributed to a near tripling of the agency's sales, with 2001 figures of $34 million rising to $100 million in 2006.

Preferred Properties also takes advantage of technology and has created an exceptional online experience for buyers and sellers. The agency's Web site, www.preferredprop.com, has been designed to enhance the buying and selling process by offering a property search function in which users can search virtually all listings in Western North Carolina, a luxury homes section specifically for homes listed at $500,000 and above, and a "Preferred Cart" feature that allows users to keep track of the properties they're interested in and email them to their broker with the push of a button. The easy-to-navigate site allows buyers to take a closer look at the beautiful and unique lifestyle that awaits them in Asheville . . . a place Preferred Properties proudly calls home. ❖

photo by tim barnwell

▲ The beauty of the Blue Ridge Mountains is unsurpassed, offering endless recreational activities that are enjoyed year-round. If your perfect home is one with a mountain view, Preferred Properties' brokers can help make that dream come true.

photo by scott indermaur

Each summer more than seventeen hundred boys from all over the United States and several foreign countries gather for fun and games at Camp Rockmont. The camp, which was established in 1956, is near the town of Black Mountain and consists of 550 secluded, privately owned acres surrounded by thousands of acres of national forest wilderness. The camp is an ideal balance between rugged mountains and level bottom land. Campers like Brett Collier from Florida can try their hand at canoeing on the camp's twenty-acre lake, playing sports on one of the four athletic fields, or sampling other activities in the gymnasium.

quick cup of joe. Something sweet to eat. A chat with a friend or

photo by mario morgado

(left page)

From pastries to panini, Rachel Smith serves it up with flair at City Bakery Café. From two locations, at 88 Charlotte Street and 60 Biltmore Avenue, the family-owned City Bakery Cafés offer delectable menus of freshly made artisan breads and pastries ranging from scones and muffins to pies and cakes. The cafés also serve a mouthwatering selection of sandwiches and salads for the lunchtime crowd. Catering and cakes to celebrate a wedding or other special occasion are also specialties of City Bakery.

(right page)

Downtown is a dining mecca, thanks in part to the Shastri family, who took a risk and brought culinary art to an area on the verge of desertion. Hop into one of their establishments— the Frog Bar—for a drink before dining at the more formal Flying Frog Café downstairs. The popular bar and deli is also a destination for more casual fare, such as tapas and sandwiches.

quiet time with a book. The coffee shop is nourishment for the community.

MAKING A DIFFERENCE: dixon hughes delivers

photo by scott indermaur

▲ *(Seated)* Ed Cody, audit member, shares a story with client Bob Wernet, CEO of Deerfield Episcopal Retirement Community. *(Standing, left to right)* Dixon Hughes's Dave Kerestes and Amy Bibby; Deerfield's Robert Chandler, CFO; and Dixon Hughes tax member, Michael Rauchwarg.

Global influence. Local presence. A special combination, found right here in Asheville in Dixon Hughes PLLC, the largest accounting and advisory firm based in the Southeast. From its local beginnings in 1979, when co–chief executive officer and Western North Carolina native Ken Hughes returned to Asheville, Dixon Hughes has become one of the modern success stories of the Western Carolinas.

Though primarily a southeastern firm in terms of location and focus, some Dixon Hughes practices serve clients throughout the United States in such niches as health care, auto dealerships, financial institutions, construction and real estate, insurance, manufacturing and distribution, government, not-for-profit, and litigation support.

"Having staff with knowledge and experience in these industries gives us an edge in the caliber of advice we can offer clients," notes Mike Crawford, member in charge of the WNC Practice. "You might call it 'premium advice,' because it's advice that reflects knowledge of their particular situation."

Regardless of the formula, it is working to the point that this hometown firm now has in excess of one thousand personnel in offices in seven southeastern states, serving an array of clients not only locally, but nationally and abroad. "We're a member of Praxity," Crawford points out. "It's one of the largest associations of independent accounting firms in the world, and it enables us to assist our clients in over eighty countries. That's reach."

Dixon Hughes places tremendous importance on its people. "A key objective for us is to hire the best and brightest, then develop and retain them with training, resources, and the opportunities they need to grow professionally," says co-CEO Ken Hughes. Further illustrating this priority, Dixon

(continued on page 72)

photo by tim barnwell

▲ Ken Jackson, president of LB Jackson and Company Inc., and his Dixon Hughes advisory team strike a pose while reviewing plans for his Stafford Hills condominium neighborhood in South Asheville. *(Left to right)* James Baley, Ken Jackson, Melanie Johnson, and Michael Crawford, tax member.

◄ Dixon Hughes member Ed Cody proudly displays ribs he and firm volunteers prepared to serve as part of his Blessings & Barbeque outreach ministry to the Asheville Buncombe Community Christian Ministries' Homeless Shelter. *(Left to right)* Eric Moody, Ed Cody, John Locke, and Tina Spring.

photo by rod reilly

Dixon Hughes has become one of the modern success stories of the Western Carolinas.

The Biltmore Company's CFO Steve Watson *(center)* enjoys a relaxing moment at Biltmore's lagoon with two of his Dixon Hughes advisors, Jon Tomberlin and Michael Crawford.

photo by tim barnwell

(Dixon Hughes continued from page 71)

Hughes has defined core values around the word PEOPLE: Passion, Excellence, Optimism, Partnering, Learning, and Ethics. "We strongly believe that by constantly recognizing that our firm is only as good as our people, we will continue to enjoy success well into the future," concludes Hughes.

When not advising clients or helping them capitalize on opportunities, the professionals of Dixon Hughes spend much of their discretionary time involved with their communities. "It's in our DNA," Crawford observes. "We believe in giving back, and we do it through time, talent, and tangible resources." Dixon Hughes's staff members can be found in every nook and cranny of the cities and towns in which they work, in civic and religious organizations, leading business associations and social services campaigns, running marathons to raise charitable monies, and sponsoring seminars to promote corporate giving.

"This aspect of our culture," Crawford points out, "has the added advantage of enabling us to attract—and keep—some of the very best people in the profession. They see that in addition to providing them with professional challenges and opportunities, we value volunteerism and philanthropy, and it draws them like a magnet. By building that talent bank for the future, we achieve yet another important goal: ensuring that we're always ready to meet our clients' changing business and personal needs." ❖

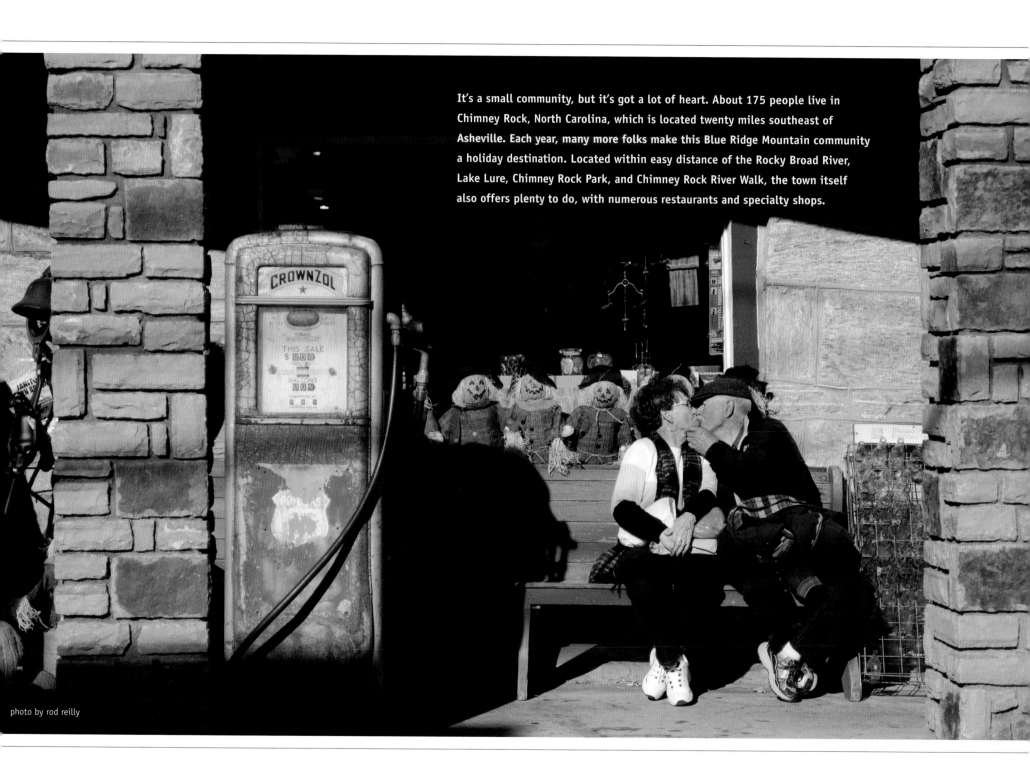

It's a small community, but it's got a lot of heart. About 175 people live in Chimney Rock, North Carolina, which is located twenty miles southeast of Asheville. Each year, many more folks make this Blue Ridge Mountain community a holiday destination. Located within easy distance of the Rocky Broad River, Lake Lure, Chimney Rock Park, and Chimney Rock River Walk, the town itself also offers plenty to do, with numerous restaurants and specialty shops.

photo by rod reilly

PADGETT & FREEMAN goes green

▲ This architectural rendition depicts the school for the Eastern Band of Cherokee Indians, scheduled for completion in 2009. The campus, designed by Padgett & Freeman Architects, is a green project, composed of environmentally responsible materials and utilizing energy-saving technology. The firm will also complete the interior design for this multimillion-dollar project.

An increasing demand for green buildings may be becoming more mainstream, but it is not so new to the team of architects and partners at Padgett & Freeman Architects in Asheville, North Carolina. Mike Freeman, Gene Edwards, and Scott Donald, partners in one of the larger architectural firms in Western North Carolina, began incorporating environmentally friendly technologies in their building designs before LEED® (Leadership in Energy and Environmental Design) was established by the U.S. Green Building Council. LEED® sets national benchmark standards for environmentally responsible building design and operating systems. In response to the increasing demand for these principles, Padgett & Freeman Architects have LEED®-accredited professionals on their staff who offer clients affordable green solutions while continuing the firm's commitment to artistic design.

"We offer this expertise along with other energy-saving technologies to our clients throughout the entire design process. We alert them to greener choices where available," Edwards explained.

The 470,000-square-foot school for the Eastern Band of Cherokee Indians, designed by the firm, is currently being built at a cost in excess of $100 million. Scheduled for completion in 2009, the innovative design will be a certified green project as well as a beautiful and functional learning institution.

For the Dogwood Project for Mission Hospitals, Padgett & Freeman Architects working in collaboration with McCulloch England Architects has designed a seven-story building to be seamlessly added to the present hospital facility. The project will provide new operating rooms and intensive-care beds, thus enabling the hospital to keep pace with present and future technologies and the growth of the area's aging population.

The Asheville High Arts Center, several projects at First Baptist Church, and the Owen Heart Center at Mission Hospitals Memorial Campus are a few of the local buildings that Padgett & Freeman Architects has designed.

"We pride ourselves on being able to tackle any size project, at any location, at any point in time," said Edwards. "We view each project as a puzzle to solve, and we use the talents of our staff to solve the puzzle and design buildings that meet the needs of our clients."

The Interior Design Department is a part of the firm's full scope of services. Basic interior design is provided as part of any project. Expanded design services such as furniture specification and procurement and custom-designed window treatments are some of the offerings from which clients may choose. The Interior Design Department has cultivated a client base independent of the architectural practice, enjoying long-term relationships with Mission Hospitals, the Biltmore Company, and a number of residential clients.

The creative team at Padgett & Freeman Architects has earned client confidence with a long history of successfully designing a diverse list of buildings that are as functional as they are beautiful. Established in 1965 by James L. Padgett, AIA, the firm remains in demand as a result of its focus on close communication with each client to create design solutions to complex and simple building challenges. ❖

photo by scott indermauer

▲ The Catherine and Charles Owen Heart Center in Asheville is a seamless addition to Mission Hospital's Memorial Campus. A creation of Padgett & Freeman, one of the largest architectural firms in Western North Carolina, the facility contains four open heart surgery suites, two vascular surgery suites, forty intensive care beds, eighty progressive care beds, an administrative suite, and a seventy-eight seat auditorium.

"We alert them to greener choices where available," Edwards explained.

hometown weaverville

Like Asheville, the small town of Weaverville six miles to the north is one of those places where you come to visit and then yearn to stay. Since its establishment in the mid-1700s, it has attracted everyone from settlers seeking a permanent home to visitors escaping the low-country heat, to modern-day pioneers in search of a spot both livable and profitable. Charming and low-key, Weaverville boasts of plenty to do and places to stay, from day spas to historic B&Bs like the Inn on Main Street, run by Dan and Nancy Ward. Likewise, Kathleen Gibbs, founder of downtown's Miya Gallery, discovered in Weaverville the perfect spot for her many beautiful creations, as well as the work of established and emerging artists and artisans. Among the town's many wonderful restaurants, the Stoney Knob Café continues to bring a touch of Greek to the scene. Established in 1962 by Gus and Minnie Dermas, sons John and Yotty now run the family business. Residents also relish the town's easy livability, well-kept neighborhoods, attentive town government, and natural beauty. In fact, the heart of the town just very well may be Lake Louise Park, a focal point for a variety of outdoor activities ranging from the aerobic to the contemplative.

photo by alan s. weiner

Weaverville is a place to relax, a place to enjoy life.

BEVERLY-HANKS & ASSOCIATES: elevating the real estate experience

▲ Beverly Hanks & Associates represents more than thirty new home communities with amenities and price points to suit any lifestyle. From luxurious estates to mountain getaways, this firm can help you find the perfect place to call home.

For more than three decades, the unwavering goal of Beverly-Hanks & Associates has been to make every aspect of buying or selling real property as smooth as possible for its clientele. From the introductory handshake to the receipt of the keys, the customer enjoys a level of service unmatched in Western North Carolina.

The cornerstone for this philosophy was laid when former competitors George Beverly and Neal Hanks Sr. joined forces in 1976 to create a firm that would exceed clients' expectations. "They were both from business backgrounds and envisioned an opportunity to distinguish their company with a progressive, service-oriented consultative approach to real estate marketing and sales," stated Neal Hanks Jr., president of Beverly-Hanks & Associates and second generation at the helm of the firm.

The success enjoyed by Beverly-Hanks is a direct result of the mission to provide peerless customer service. Under the visionary leadership of Neal Hanks Jr., the firm has further

(continued on page 82)

photo by rod reilly

▲ Under the visionary leadership of Neal Hanks, Jr., the second generation of one of the founding partners, Beverly-Hanks & Associates is continuing to strengthen its position as an industry leader in the Western North Carolina real estate market.

◀ Asheville's downtown condominium communities offer contemporary architecture and a variety of amenities which can be enjoyed in a historic setting with stunning views of the city and mountains.

photo by rod reilly

The success enjoyed by Beverly-Hanks is a direct result of the mission to provide peerless customer service.

If space with a view is your pleasure, Asheville is the place to be. Beverly-Hanks builds long-term relationships with its home buyers, helping them move from first home to family homestead to retirement retreat.

photo by rod reilly

(Beverly-Hanks & Associates continued from page 81)

strengthened its position as industry leader in marketing real estate in Western North Carolina. Hanks has responded to today's consumer preferences by providing a one-stop shopping experience. Buyers may begin their property search at their convenience by visiting www.beverly-hanks.com. The Beverly-Hanks Web site allows consumers to view residential or commercial property, prequalify or apply for a mortgage, search new home communities, and personally select a real estate professional that will best meet their needs.

Most importantly, Hanks has carefully expanded the company to more than three hundred full-time brokers averaging thirteen years experience each. These professionals currently work from seven offices and a score of new home community sales centers located in Buncombe, Henderson, and Haywood counties.

A commitment to ongoing training for all agents provides customers with the knowledge needed to make informed decisions. "We believe if we can attract and retain the best agents, and provide an environment for them to be successful, then they will in turn deliver unparalleled service to our customers," says Hanks. To this end, the firm employs a full-time director of training who coordinates over three hundred hours of courses annually.

A corollary attribute of the firm's customer-service focus is the Beverly-Hanks commitment to make a significant difference in the communities it serves. Whether swinging hammers on a Habitat for Humanity home, volunteering with the Chamber of Commerce, or helping out in schools or churches, the fingerprints of Beverly-Hanks agents are evident throughout the cities and towns where the agents live. "Western North Carolina has been very good to us," says Debbie Williams, general manager. "It is our genuine pleasure to give back to the communities where we live and work."

A premiere sales team, unparalleled training, and a companywide belief in giving back contribute to the success of the firm. The most valuable result of these attributes is the long-lasting relationships forged between agents and their customers. The course of these relationships can be traced on a map as

(continued on page 84)

photo by rod reilly

▲ Beverly-Hanks is dedicated to making a significant difference in the lives of its neighbors. A favorite charitable activity for the Beverly-Hanks team is to lend dozens of helping hands in the building of homes for Habitat for Humanity.

◀ Family and outdoor fun are hallmarks of life in Asheville. While the mountain setting and climate beckon you to enjoy some of the simpler things in life, modern conveniences, fine dining and the arts are within close proximity.

photo by rod reilly

{Beverly-Hanks & Associates continued from page 83}

clients move into their first home in one neighborhood, move their growing family into another home, and settle in another home years later as empty nesters, assisted every time by their own Beverly-Hanks agent.

Many of these moves are chronicled by testimonials that flow into the Beverly-Hanks office on a daily basis—prose tributes that speak to the tight bond that forms between agent and client. "This will be our tenth move, and we have worked with as many Realtors," wrote one client. "Our Beverly-Hanks agent is by far the best we have ever had the pleasure of working with." Another client wrote, "My agent is a true professional in every respect, extremely knowledgeable, totally dedicated, and leaves no stone unturned to serve the client well." Another wrote, "As a first-time buyer, I was amazed at how our agent made the whole process easy and comfortable. She put all the lingo into words that I could understand, and I never once had any doubts about my purchase."

Small wonder that so many clients rely on Beverly-Hanks for residential real estate sales and purchases.

Through the Beverly-Hanks network affiliation with Leading Real Estate Companies of the World, the firm is able to help individuals, families, and businesses with their relocation efforts, assisting in home listing and purchase, planning and moving household goods, mortgage options, rental choices, employment information, coordination of temporary or extended living, and home protection.

Builders and developers of new communities have come to depend on Beverly-Hanks's vast knowledge of the community and housing trends, enabling them to build homes that will meet the needs of today's consumer. "We can help them to plan and prepare a product that the market's asking for," says Hanks, "and then we work with them all the way through the advertising and marketing stages to the actual sales of the homes."

Beverly-Hanks & Associates currently represents more than thirty new home communities, with amenities and price points to meet the needs of each of our customers. "All of this, and more," adds Hanks, "is why a relationship with Beverly-Hanks 'exceeds expectations.'" ❖

photo by rod reilly

▲ Asheville is a place where neighbors still enjoy spending an afternoon or evening relaxing on the porch. With the help of the Beverly-Hanks relocation team, individuals, families, and businesses can quickly feel right at home in their new surroundings.

Springtime in Asheville provides hikers and road trippers with plenty of opportunities to marvel at nature's exuberant renewal of color. Western North Carolina is so varied in its elevations and terrain that, whether out in the field or inside the North Carolina Arboretum, flower enthusiasts can catch blooms from March through the end of June.

the world upon a stage

photo by alan s. weiner

When Asheville performers take to the stage, they really know how to put on a show. From classics by Shakespeare to modern works by the likes of Arthur Miller, Asheville's actors deliver a full calendar of performances guaranteed to delight audiences of all interests. In addition to productions by local talent, touring companies also bring their productions to Asheville stages. Those stages include multiple venues, indoors and out, that give audiences and actors a chance to get up close and personal—from black-box stages like that at the "BeBe" and 35below theatres to the five-hundred-seat Diana Wortham Theatre at Pack Place to the unique State Theatre of North Carolina known as Flat Rock Playhouse. Among the presentations in the area's year-round repertoire are comedies, tragedies, histories, dramas, musicals, mysteries, kids' shows, and so much more. For instance, in addition to its main season productions, the North Carolina Stage Company presents locally created performances, special events, and an almost-anything-goes open venue known as No Shame Theatre. During the summer months, productions in neighboring towns include an outdoor portrayal of local Native American history at Mountainside Theatre in Cherokee as well as presentations about the area's mountain heritage by the Southern Appalachian Repertory Company over in Mars Hill.

photo by mario morgado

DOUBLETREE BILTMORE HOTEL: a tradition of hospitality

▲ Guests checking in to the Doubletree Biltmore Hotel are treated to Doubletree's trademark chocolate-chip cookies, plus a piece of Asheville history. The museum-worthy contents in the cabinets that line the lobby's walls include Vanderbilt family photographs, beautiful old china, colorful ice-cream molds, and old-time dairy gear. They tell the story of how the home of Biltmore Dairy Farms became one of Asheville's leading hotels.

The lobby of the Doubletree Biltmore Hotel is a place of great charm and character. Here guests are treated at check-in to Doubletree's trademark chocolate chip cookies. They are also treated to something less expected: a storied piece of Asheville history.

This history lies in the wooden cabinets that line the lobby's walls. Their museum-worthy contents—family photographs, beautiful old china, colorful ice-cream molds, and old-time dairy gear—tell the exceptional story of how one of Asheville's leading hotels came to be.

The story begins in the late 1880s when George W. Vanderbilt created Biltmore Dairy Farms. Originally the milk produced was for consumption at his private estate, Biltmore. When the farms began producing a surplus, he started giving the milk to local hospitals. By the century's turn, he was bottling and delivering it to homes. At its peak, Biltmore Dairy Farms had more than 175 home delivery routes, its name synonymous with the very best milk and ice cream available.

Meanwhile, in New York, the recently founded Biltmore Hotel was gaining a luxurious reputation. When the dairy farms were eventually sold, it was decided that the name of Biltmore should once again grace the façade of a hotel— except this time in Asheville, not New York.

The former seat of the dairy farm's operations became the site of a new hotel. That elegant lobby, where guests relax today, was once a part of the ice-cream manufacturing area. A number of years, extensive remodeling, and a major renovation later, the site emerged as the Doubletree Bilt-more Hotel, a member of the Hilton chain. Today it is managed by Biltmore Farms Hotels, which also manages Quality Inn and Suites Biltmore South, Residence Inn Biltmore, and Sleep Inn Biltmore.

Located in the historic Biltmore Village area, the Doubletree Biltmore Hotel sits less than one mile from downtown and one block from Biltmore Estate. Its 160 rooms are characterized by their well-appointed comfort, featuring Doubletree's lush Sweet Dreams bedding, free wireless, and an oversized work desk with ergonomic chair.

In 2007, the hotel opened a new chapter in its history. In response to requests for additional luxury accommodations, the hotel embarked on a yearlong expansion project. The result will be a five-story concierge tower with luxury suites, expanded meeting spaces that can seat up to 275 people, a state-of-the-art fitness center, an indoor pool with Whirlpool® Spa, and a grand terrace with an outdoor fireplace.

Whether dairy farm or hotel, all the businesses that carry the Biltmore name take that honor seriously, which sometimes calls for extraordinary action. In 2004 when hurricanes Frances and Ivan flooded Biltmore Village, the Doubletree put together a cookout for everyone working on cleanup. The hotel also allowed a flooded restaurant to use its kitchen to keep its catering business going, which in turn saved the restaurant from having to close permanently. George W. Vanderbilt would have applauded that kind of community responsibility. It is the spirit of the Vanderbilt tradition. ❖

photo by alan s. weiner

▲ Located in the historic Biltmore Village area, the Doubletree Biltmore Hotel sits less than one mile from downtown. Its 160 rooms are characterized by their well-appointed comfort, featuring Doubletree's lush Sweet Dreams bedding, free wireless, and an oversized work desk with ergonomic chair. In 2007 the hotel embarked on a yearlong expansion project. The result will be a five-story concierge tower with luxury suites, expanded meeting spaces, a state-of-the-art fitness center, an indoor pool with Whirlpool® Spa, and a grand terrace with an outdoor fireplace.

The Doubletree Biltmore Hotel sits less than one mile from downtown and one block from Biltmore Estate.

true love and home-grown tomatoes

"There's only two things that money can't buy,
True love and home-grown tomatoes."
(Lyric by John Denver)

Laurey Masterton (right) manages to have both. True love for her business—cooking—and home-grown tomatoes, beans, corn, squash, peas, and all the other fresh vegetables she buys from local farmers and uses at Laurey's Catering (Yum) and Gourmet-to-Go.

She moved to Asheville to participate in Outward Bound, but soon realized that was not to be her life's work, so she started a catering business from her apartment. "My parents founded the Blueberry Hill Inn in Vermont and wrote the Blueberry Hill cookbooks, so it seemed like a logical choice. It worked fine for a while, then the health department caught up with me. I had to either get out, or get legit. So I opened the restaurant.

"I got interested in locally grown veggies when I read Alice Waters's book. She said we should all know who grows our food. So when a farmer asked if he could grow vegetables for me, I was delighted. We went through the seed catalogue, and that was the beginning. Now I have about twenty farmers who grow veggies for us. One farmer brings in what I always refer to as 'cute baby squash.' I've done it so long, he now lists it that way on his invoices. We also serve locally supplied beef, pork, eggs, and flowers."

Laurey is passionately and officially committed to sustainable farming, which involves creating profitable local markets so farmers can stay on their land and pass it along to the next generation. "Buying local has really caught on. There's a farmers' market across the street from the restaurant, there are tailgate markets everywhere, and lots of chefs and specialty restaurants now rely on local products."

It's all there in her mission, which says in part, "Our aim is to run a profitable business, use the very best ingredients available from local sources . . . . and to have fun while we do what we do." Mission accomplished.

Serving real food prepared with real love.

Laurey Masterton
Chef, Restaurant Owner

Laurey is passionately and officially committed to sustainable farming.

LASTING TIES: morosani & associates investing in the future

photo by tim barnwell

George W. Morosani & Associates has served Western North Carolina with commercial, industrial, and residential properties and property management since 1969. President George Morosani (seated) and his staff—Lisa Stephens, Curtis Burge, Jim Diaz, and Andrew Huska—are dedicated to finding and developing new properties.

In a world of instant coffee, instant messaging, and instant gratification, it is refreshing to find a company placing equal emphasis on current success and long-term rewards. That is exactly what George W. Morosani & Associates is all about.

"When I first came to Asheville in the late 1960s," said president and broker-in-charge George Morosani, "there were many residential real estate agents, but very few who dealt with commercial properties. Closings don't happen fast—just the very nature of commercial and industrial real estate. Negotiations can take months or even years, but the rewards are there for those willing to learn the business, the market, and wait."

Morosani started with a warehousing business in 1969. He had more than five acres under one roof, but needed only half the space. In the process of finding tenants for the other half, he learned the ins and outs of leasing and managing commercial properties. Now, Morosani & Associates manages about 1.3 million square feet and brokers numerous other commercial properties each year.

One unique feature of Morosani & Associates is its extensive inventory of company-owned properties. While most real estate brokers sell or lease inventory owned by their clients, Morosani works from his own inventory much of the time. "I keep my eyes open so I know who has extra space or land and who might need it. Also, I encourage my staff to invest in real estate, as over the years, it will not only provide a comfortable living, but a nice nest egg for retirement as well. The ownership element gives our brokers a unique knowledge of the market."

(continued on page 96)

photo by alan s. weiner

▲ Curtis Burge, Andrew Huska, George Morosani, Lisa Stephens, and Jim Diaz examine blueprints for Forest Center North, a multi-use property designed by architect Robert Griffin. The facility was built and is owned by George W. Morosani & Associates.

▼ One of the latest Morosani developments, this eighty-thousand-square-foot mixed-use facility is proposed for 2130 Hendersonville Road. The ground floor will contain a variety of retail areas, while the upper three floors will provide office space.

It is refreshing to find a company placing equal emphasis on current success and long-term rewards.

(Morosani & Associates continued from page 95)

Morosani has assembled a young staff trained and dedicated to finding and developing new properties while carrying on the brokerage business into the future. Included in this select group are Lisa Stephens, broker and leasing expert; Andrew Huska, a semiretired real estate broker; Jim Diaz, commercial broker and investor; and Curtis Burge, commercial broker and investor. Diaz and Burge are members of the CCIM Institute as Certified Commercial Investment Members, recognized experts in commercial real estate brokerage, leasing, asset management, valuation, and investment analysis.

Morosani's belief in long-term relationships is evident in his involvement in the Asheville community. One of his first associations was spearheading the Jaycees project to build 180 low-income housing units in the early 1970s. This project enabled him to branch out on his own, building fourteen apartment complexes over the next ten years. He continues to own and manage them to this day.

Another long-term partnership is with Junior Achievement. In 1977, Morosani helped them find space for their activities—teaching high school students practical skills to function in the business world—and has since served on their board for over thirty years. Morosani has equally lasting relationships with the Better Business Bureau and the Civitan Club. He is also an active member of the Land-of-the-Sky Regional Council Board of Directors as its Buncombe County Economic Development Representative, and the Buncombe County Board of Adjustment, serving each organization for more than ten years.

"My favorite part of this business is developing something from nothing: buy the land, construct the building, lease it, and manage it," Morosani said.

Evidence that he continues to do just that is the four-story, eighty-thousand-square-foot retail and office center he is developing on Hendersonville Road at Rosscraggon Road. The building is in the South Asheville/Airport area, a hot location. There's no doubt that as more opportunities open up, Morosani & Associates will be there promoting and investing in Asheville's future, as it has since 1969. ❖

photo by tim barnwell

▲ Lisa Stephens, Curtis Burge, George Morosani, Andrew Huska, and Jim Diaz visit Piedmont Interstate Industrial Warehouse. This recent 250,000-square-foot acquisition is typical of the kind of property in which George W. Morosani & Associates specializes.

M Most people who are familiar with downtown Asheville easily recognize the Buncombe County Courthouse and City Hall. The courthouse was completed in 1928 and is one of the most extravagant in the state. And City Hall is a colorful, massive, art-deco masterpiece. However, sometimes it takes a new perspective to really appreciate what has become so familiar.

INSURANCE SERVICE OF ASHEVILLE: practice makes perfect

photo by lloyd hammarlund

▲ Their names aren't on the door, though these "starting five" ISA owner/officers are totally committed to the agency's goals and tradition of providing top value to insureds for half a century. *(Left to right)* Jim Stickney, president; Jonathan Nelson, vice president, commercial lines; Sam Stickney, senior vice president; Mary Alice Arthur, vice president, administration; and Sharon Robbins, vice president, life, health, and employee benefits.

Balancing tradition with innovation isn't easy, but it's an art that Insurance Service of Asheville (ISA) has nearly perfected. Established in 1958, ISA's distinguished past and reputation as one of Asheville's most dependable full-service insurance firms are the foundation for a bright future. Continually evolving to meet the needs of a growing community, the agency maintains the traditions that have made it successful while readily adapting to changing times.

"We're a family-owned and managed company, and we want to preserve our best traditions. But we recognize modern business realities and know we must also continue to be innovative," says James (Jim) Stickney IV, who assumed leadership of ISA in 2005 after his father and agency founder, James W. Stickney III, passed away.

To uphold its legacy, ISA has stayed true to the insurance products and services its clients depend on, from commercial lines and personal coverage to life, health, and employee benefits. With such a diverse repertoire, as well as the ability to take advantage of good opportunities without taking its eye off the ball, the company has been a reliable resource for individuals, families, and businesses for five decades.

The agency was built on providing exceptional value rather than salesmanship. "Our loyal customers get top priority," explains Jim. "One size does not fit all, so we match the right people and services for each client. We're here to take care of people."

That's why ISA is so active in the community—another treasured tradition. Working with such caring organizations as Hospice, The Health Adventure, and United Way, the company

photo by mario morgado

ISA vice president Sharon Robbins and senior vice president Sam Stickney enjoy an interactive lesson from The Health Adventure's Techno Man. In keeping with the agency's long-standing tradition of community service, Sam serves as The Health Adventure's chairman of the board.

and its eighteen employees consistently give back to their community. "Our quality of life here is what we make of it," says Jim, "and the charities we support complement the people and businesses we serve."

A desire to give their very best in all areas is what encourages Jim and his brother Sam, who also joined the firm in the early 1980s, to embrace those modern realities and make adjustments to the company's executive management team. "As

we've grown, we've strived to engage and empower our key employees," Sam notes. "By being open and embracing new ideas, ISA has been able to enhance services and provide innovative new products."

Throughout its history, ISA has led the way in providing protection and peace of mind for its customers. As the company looks ahead to its fiftieth anniversary in 2008, it is as much a door to the future as it is a window into the past. ❖

"By being open and embracing new ideas, ISA has been able to enhance services and provide innovative new products."

photo by scott indermaur

photo by scott indermaur

(left page)
Browse the myriad goods lining the shelves of Mast General Store in downtown Asheville, and you're sure to find something you need, or at least something you want—from candy to clothing. The original store, built in the late 1800s in Valle Crucis, was so well known for its breadth of merchandise that people often said, "If you can't buy it here, you probably don't need it."

(right page)
The color of Asheville City Hall reflects the natural clay-pink shades of the local soil. But seen from a distance, viewers may miss some of the details of this gigantic art-deco building. The octagonal roof is covered with triangular terra cotta red tiles. Between the levels of the roof are pink Georgia marble piers and rows of ornamental green and feather motifs.

photo by mario morgado

STILL BUILDING — biltmore looks to the future

▲ During April and May of each year, spring arrives with an awesome display of more than one hundred thousand tulips, daffodils, and hyacinths across Biltmore's grounds. The beds are worked and replanted three times a year, tulips in spring, bedding plants in summer, and chrysanthemums in fall.

In 1889, when George Washington Vanderbilt decided to build a mountain retreat for family and friends, he wisely chose Asheville. His palatial home, Biltmore, boasts 250 rooms, an indoor pool, a bowling alley, and priceless art and antiques. From the beginning, Vanderbilt played a key part in encouraging economic development in Asheville and the entire Western North Carolina region. That spirit continues today under the leadership of his family, who opened Biltmore to the public in 1930.

Through the years, Biltmore has expanded its use of the popular estate grounds. The challenge of keeping the estate preserved and open to the public was met with goals of visitation growth, and other opportunities for revenue. The family made diversification a priority during the oil crises in the 1970s. If guests couldn't afford gas to drive to the French Renaissance chateau, then Biltmore needed to bring it to them.

In the late 1970s, Biltmore began to experiment with wine making. The winery opened in 1985 and is now the most visited winery in the United States. Producing approximately 150,000 cases a year, Biltmore wines are distributed to twelve states and the District of Columbia.

Beyond the estate and gardens, Biltmore has created Biltmore for Your Home, the product licensing division of the company, to offer products inspired by the estate. Items such as furniture, hardwood floors, paints, cookware, bedroom furnishings, and plants are part of the program. Partners include respected companies such as Belk, Magnussen, Anderson Hardwood Floors, and Olympic Paints.

In 2001, Inn on Biltmore Estate, a 213-room four-star hotel, opened on the property to give visitors a taste of what it might have been like to be a guest of the Vanderbilts. With people staying multiple days, the estate offers outdoor activities including hiking trails, fly-fishing, carriage rides, horseback riding, calm-water rafting, and biking across the eight-thousand-acre estate.

While the estate will always remain Biltmore's flagship and an oasis for more than 1 million guests per year, the brand now reaches customers across the United States. That growth translates into preservation of this National Historic Landmark.

"Part of our core value that is instilled in us is this whole idea that we should make a profit to preserve Biltmore rather than profit from the estate," said Jerry Douglas, senior vice president of marketing and sales at the Biltmore Company. "That's what we strive for every day."

In other words, Biltmore has become a successful national brand, a private company with $130 million in annual revenue and growing sales. This makes it unique as a historic landmark because it remains completely self-sufficient, receiving no governmental funding.

While other historic sites are looking to the past, Biltmore is looking to an optimistic future. No doubt George Washington Vanderbilt would be pleased. ❖

The most-visited winery in this country is not in Napa Valley, it is at Biltmore. The award-winning wines are produced and bottled on the property in a nintey-thousand-square-foot, state-of-the-art facility which opened to guests in 1985. It is housed in a converted dairy barn, designed by the architect of Biltmore House.

While other historic sites are looking to the past, Biltmore is looking to an optimistic future.

all photos by mario morgado

If Paris is the city of light, then Asheville, which is called the Paris of the South, is the city of music. Live music is definitely drawing locals and visitors downtown. There are more than fifty clubs and other entertainment venues listing live performances. And let's not forget the music festivals that are held each summer. As country-pop Grammy-winner Shelby Lynne said recently, "Asheville is definitely a music town."

BILTMORE FARMS COMMERCIAL: planning for tomorrow

Biltmore Park offers residents a vibrant, family-friendly atmosphere. At the heart of the community is Town Square, which encompasses a mix of shops, restaurants, a YMCA, entertainment, housing, and Class-A office space. Corporate Technology Center is home to many regional, national, and international headquarters.

Stroll through Biltmore Park's Town Square, and you will see the innovation and vision of Biltmore Farms Commercial at work. Main Street is reborn in this forty-two-acre urban village, the largest mixed-use district outside of Asheville's downtown. The thriving community center holds a mix of restaurants, shops, and state-of-the-art office space—their presence a testament to the incredible range found in this company's portfolio of properties and services.

Leasing, property management, development, and project management are the firm's core competencies. With a culture dedicated to fulfilling the exact needs of each client professionally, punctually, and seamlessly, Biltmore Farms Commercial helps companies and individuals maximize the return on their commercial real-estate investment.

Recently, four of the company's commercial properties received the National Commercial Real Estate Customer Service Award for Excellence—which is often referred to as the "A List" Award—from CEL & Associates Inc. The announcement stated, "When compared to other properties throughout the country, Biltmore Commercial Real Estate (Biltmore Farms Commercial) has properties with tenant satisfaction scores among the highest in the nation." The company has won six previous A List Awards.

As a member of the Biltmore Farms family of companies, Biltmore Farms Commercial is charged with carrying forward a century-long tradition of excellence, quality, and the kind of smart, sustainable planning that makes a community great. ❖

Leasing, property management, development, and project management are the firm's core competencies.

Once you spend a day at the shops at Biltmore Village, you may never go back to a mall. Built in the late 1890s as a planned community just outside the Biltmore Estate, the retail complex is distinguished by the old-world charm of its nineteenth-century architecture, brick sidewalks, and quaint, tree-lined streets. Its range of retailers has earned Biltmore Village an international reputation for rare antiques, specialty art and crafts, top-of-the-line clothing and jewelry, and nature-related items and outdoor gear. Eight restaurants provide shoppers with welcome respite at breakfast, lunch, and dinner.

photo by scott indrmaur

BILTMORE FARMS COMMUNITIES: a natural harmony

George W. Vanderbilt's commitment to maintaining the natural beauty and quality of life in Western North Carolina is evident in each of the Biltmore Farms Communities, including Biltmore Forest, Biltmore Park, Biltmore Lake, and the latest, The Ramble Biltmore Forest. Longmeadow Park at The Ramble is a twelve-and-a-quarter-acre park with native plantings and open space for all the residents to enjoy.

George W. Vanderbilt's commitment to maintaining the natural beauty and quality of life in Western North Carolina is evident in each of the Biltmore Farms Communities, including Biltmore Forest, Biltmore Park, Biltmore Lake, and the latest, The Ramble Biltmore Forest.

When George Vanderbilt created Biltmore Estate, he hired landscape architect Frederick Law Olmsted—who designed New York's Central Park—to sculpt its gardens and grounds. A similar ethos and principles of conservation were closely followed in Biltmore Forest. A masterpiece of natural beauty, Biltmore Forest set the benchmark for all future Biltmore Farms Communities.

Biltmore Park offers residents a vibrant, family-friendly atmosphere. At the heart of the community is Town Square, which encompasses a mix of shops, restaurants, a YMCA, entertainment, and housing as well as Class-A office space. Corporate Technology Center is home to many regional, national, and international headquarters.

Biltmore Lake sits on the shores of a sixty-two-acre lake. Framed by rolling hills and mountain views, the community recalls the spirit of a simpler time, with wide streets and inviting parks. Its homes combine old-fashioned quality workmanship with modern conveniences.

In both Biltmore and Central Park, Olmsted created a "wild garden" called the Ramble. Biltmore Farms' latest community, The Ramble, pays tribute to Olmsted with a design that invites exploration and time spent outdoors. Ample parks and gardens adorn this luxurious woodland community, nestled onto Ducker Mountain's northern face.

Each Biltmore Farms Community carries forward the Vanderbilt tradition of sustainability, quality, and excellence. ❖

A masterpiece of natural beauty, Biltmore Forest set the benchmark for all future Biltmore Farms Communities.

What better place than the Botanical Gardens at Asheville to recharge your body, mind, and spirit? The Sunshine Meadow is the scene for a series of body-based activities offered on alternate Thursdays and designed to reconnect body and soul. Tai Chi is just part of this interesting series. The Botanical Gardens are dedicated to preserving and protecting native plants and offer a wide range of educational workshops. A sampling includes an Introduction to Birding, the Annual Wildflower Walk, Stonescaping for Your Yard, and their most popular workshop, Analyzing Your Mountain Homestead. Entrance to the gardens is free, but donations are always appreciated.

BILTMORE FARMS HOMES: built for a lifetime

Biltmore Farms Homes offers a number of styles ranging from French to English and Craftsman to Classical. Each residence, like this one at Cedar Rock in Biltmore Lake, combines classic charm with modern conveniences and features open layouts, light-filled interiors, wide porches, and other amenities.

Since the 1800s, when George W. Vanderbilt commissioned the building of his famed estate, the name Biltmore has long been associated with extraordinary homes. Biltmore Farms Homes carries forward that tradition. A part of Biltmore Farms, the company Vanderbilt founded in 1897, this homebuilding firm is known for creating homes of exceptional comfort, beauty, and quality.

Biltmore Farms Homes encompasses a number of styles ranging from French to English and Craftsman to Classical. The designs are chosen to fit perfectly against the beauty of the Blue Ridge Mountains.

Each home combines classic charm with modern convenience, and features open layouts, light-filled interiors, wide porches, and other amenities. From the placement of the home on the site to the installation of the crown molding, every detail is carefully considered and artfully executed by the Biltmore Farms construction team.

A highlight of the homebuilding experience comes with a visit to the MyBiltmoreHome Studio. Here clients go about creating the home of their dreams. The studio is filled with wonderful options for the new homeowner to consider, including floor samples, lighting design, tile styles and colors, even kitchen and bathroom fixtures. Choose a treatment for a media room, add an at-home office—the possibilities are limitless.

Each Biltmore Farms Home is constructed to reflect the Vanderbilt family's unwavering commitment to fine craftsmanship. These are not just well-built houses; they are homes built for a lifetime. ❖

From the placement of the home on the site to the installation of the crown molding, every detail is carefully considered.

photo by scott indermaur

Golfers have enjoyed the 18-hole, Donald Ross–designed Asheville Municipal Golf Course and its beautiful mountain setting since 1927. Both challenging and fun, the course features a par-36, wide-open front nine and a par-36 back nine with narrow fairways. The course is open to the public, as weather permits, but requires tee times. Memberships and rental clubs are available, and there is an on-site clubhouse complete with concessions and a pro shop.

BILTMORE FARMS, LLC: a growing tradition

Biltmore Lake lies only fifteen minutes from downtown. ▷
The lakeside community embodies the old-fashioned
virtues of simplicity and natural harmony. At the
community's center is this sixty-two-acre lake, framed by
rolling hills, breathtaking mountain views, and a
vibrant community center.

George W. Vanderbilt was that rare sort of individual who could take something good and leave it better. He first began acquiring land in Asheville in 1887. On this land he built his famed Biltmore Estate and, in so doing, introduced the principles of sustainable community to Western North Carolina.

Biltmore Farms was born of Vanderbilt's vision. Founded in 1897, Biltmore Farms has become a guiding force in land management and community development in Western North Carolina. What began as the agricultural arm of Vanderbilt's estate has become a diverse array of companies, each serving an essential function in bringing economic and cultural prosperity to this region. Included in this family of companies is Biltmore Farms Communities, Biltmore Farms Homes, Biltmore Farms Commercial, and Biltmore Farms Hotels.

The historic Town of Biltmore Forest was the first community developed by Biltmore Farms. Beloved today for its immense trees and naturally landscaped streets, Biltmore Forest set a precedent for the company's future projects, which include three of the region's premier mixed-use master-planned communities, Biltmore Park, Biltmore Lake, and The Ramble.

Combining beautiful residential neighborhoods with a developing Town Square, Biltmore Park offers its residents the opportunity to live, work, and play in one location. With its greenway trails, great recreational opportunities, as well as shopping and dining options, it's little wonder that Biltmore Park has become one of Asheville's most favored addresses.

In addition to its Corporate Technology Center, home to Volvo North America Construction headquarters, Biltmore Park Town Square is Asheville's first urban village and the largest mixed-use district outside of the city's downtown. Boasting an intriguing mix of stores, restaurants, and state-of-the-art office space, Town Square is one of several properties expertly managed and leased by Biltmore Farms Commercial, which specializes in retail and commercial development.

Biltmore Lake lies only fifteen minutes from downtown. This lakeside community embodies the old-fashioned virtues of simplicity and natural harmony. At the community's center is a sixty-two-acre lake, framed by rolling hills and breathtaking mountain views, and a vibrant community center.

Lying within the southern boundary of the Town of Biltmore Forest, The Ramble returned Biltmore Farms to its roots. Sculpted into the woodlands of Ducker Mountain, this luxurious community features a wealth of scenic parks, gardens, and green spaces that pay tribute to Vanderbilt and Frederick Law Olmsted, landscape architect of Biltmore Estate.

Each of these communities provide a wonderful backdrop for the showcase homes of Biltmore Farms Homes. Working with clients across Western North Carolina, Biltmore Farms builds quality homes that perfectly complement their mountain surroundings.

Meanwhile, visitors to Asheville will immediately recognize the Biltmore name and standard of hospitality in Doubletree Biltmore Hotel, Quality Inn and Suites Biltmore South, Residence Inn Biltmore, and Sleep Inn Biltmore.

For over a century, and across its many enterprises, Biltmore Farms has carried forth George Vanderbilt's wish, that only the very best products and services be allowed to carry the name of Biltmore. ❖

▲ George W. Vanderbilt was an individual who could take something good and leave it better. He first began acquiring land in Asheville in 1887. Biltmore Farms LLC was born of Vanderbilt's vision. Founded in 1897, the company has become a guiding force in land management and community development in Western North Carolina.

Biltmore Farms has become a guiding force in land management and community development in Western North Carolina.

photo by tim barnwell

photo by mario morgado

(far left)

Drum circles have a long and varied history, some traditional, some cultural, some religious. A community drum circle like the one in Pritchard Park in downtown Asheville is designed to allow everyone to experience the forces of rhythmic entertainment. When the circle works as a team, everyone benefits, and the energy flows.

(center)

When checking out the sights in a new city or visiting some of your favorite places, it's best to have a good vantage point. And what could be better than a moving observation post that magically walks you by everything there is to see?

(right)

The secret to antiquing is time, patience, an open mind, and, of course, choices. Lots and lots of choices. Asheville offers the perfect combination of these elements. Antique shops are everywhere. Whether you're looking for furniture, jewelry, decorative objects, lighting, fine art, or rugs, a day of browsing is sure to turn up a treasure or two.

CITY OF ASHEVILLE: quality services for a quality life

photo by scott indermaur

Visits to the WNC Nature Center are fun, educational, and memorable. The Nature Center is a living exhibit of native southern Appalachian plants and animals. Its goal is to interpret the natural environment and foster understanding of the ecosystem.

In a community renowned for its extraordinary quality of life, the City of Asheville works with residents to ensure that this will always be a great place to call home.

As the seat of Buncombe County and a regional hub for business, health care, culture, and entertainment, a good portion of the city's services are focused on keeping infrastructure operating safely and efficiently.

But beyond streets and buildings, the city works to keep Asheville a place of great natural beauty through its award-winning parks and recreation department, which maintains more than fifty public parks, a collection of community centers, and a comprehensive program of athletics and cultural activities for residents of all ages. The city also runs the popular and challenging eighteen-hole municipal golf course, designed by renowned architect Donald Ross, which has been a part of the landscape since 1927. The Western North Carolina Nature Center is also a city property. Once a beloved forty-acre zoo, the center has been transformed into an animal sanctuary, nature lab, and educational farm through the efforts of city and citizens.

City responsibilities include development of Asheville's growing system of greenways, slated to become fourteen corridors with twenty-nine miles of trails that connect the places where people live, work, and play. Uniquely, the city also organizes the exciting three-day Bele Chere, a celebration of "beautiful living" that fills Asheville's downtown streets with art, music, and some three hundred thousand festivalgoers each year.

Looking after Asheville's future is a collaborative effort between citizens and city government. Through city-hosted community forums on specific issues, residents have the opportunity to form a consensus and make recommendations to the city council. Additionally, the city employs a liaison to address the needs of neighborhood associations and to help, rather than hinder, efforts to maintain the historic character and integrity of the community.

Clean water is another hallmark of life in Asheville, whether it is for consumption or recreation. That's why the city places great importance on management of its pristine watershed lake, converging rivers, and stormwater systems, addressing problems as they arise and working to prevent concerns of the future.

An environmentally cleaner future was the concern that led the city council to a 2007 decision to adopt carbon emission reduction goals and set Leadership in Energy and Environmental Design standards for all city buildings built thereafter. Being mindful of the safety of residents today and tomorrow is what guides the efforts of the city's fully accredited police department, an agency of some four hundred officers and volunteers, and fire department, whose special duties include swift water rescue and regional hazardous material response for the region.

Amid the beauty that is the Blue Ridge Mountains, the government and citizens of Asheville will keep working together to ensure their community remains a special place. ❖

The City of Asheville is committed to keeping ours a safe city with safe neighborhoods. Both the Asheville Police Department and Fire and Rescue Department are fully accredited. They protect the lives, property, and environment of Asheville residents and visitors.

photo by scott indermaur

Looking after Asheville's future is a collaborative effort between citizens and city government.

Bouchon, a French bistro in Asheville, is a world away from Lyon, France, where owner Michel Baudouin grew up in the countryside. Yet after years as a successful restaurateur in Texas, Baudouin feels most at home in his cozy cafe that features French comfort food, the repast he remembers from boyhood. The Baudouin family shows affection for the community through creative charity events such as Yappy Hour for the American Humane Society and Dining Out for Life, an AIDS benefit. The popular bistro is busy, but this chef claims his work is play. "We offer French fare without the airfare," he said. "The only thing we don't offer here is attitude."

(above)

It may look like the entrance to a hotel, but it is actually a lot more. In the late 1880s George W. Vanderbilt created Biltmore Dairy Farms. Originally the milk produced was for consumption at his private estate, Biltmore. When the farms began producing a surplus, he gave it to local hospitals. By the turn of the century, he was bottling and delivering it to homes. At its peak, Biltmore Dairy Farms had more than 175 home delivery routes. The former dairy farm is currently the site of the Doubletree Biltmore Hotel.

(left)

During the spring and summer months, the Blue Ridge Mountains surrounding Asheville truly come alive, bursting with color and brimming with beguiling wildlife. At Mountain Air Country Club, the community's resident naturalist can take families on amazing daily adventures, guiding them as they traverse the nature and hiking trails of the old-growth forest and enlightening them with creative recreational family programs. Here, two of Mountain Air's younger residents encounter a lovely waterfall while taking a hike. Armed with their trusty binoculars, these two little ladies are undoubtedly seeing nature in a new light, getting up close to the beauty that surrounds them and acquiring a new appreciation for the environment.

BEVERLY-HANKS MORTGAGE SERVICES — making real estate financing easy and convenient

photo by rod reilly

▲ Beverly-Hanks Mortgage Services make it easy to buy a home. Located just down the hall from the real estate offices, the mortgage services division provides the financing options you need when purchasing property.

everly-Hanks Mortgage Services makes the home buying process seamless and enjoyable. "We are dedicated to exceeding expectations and working as a team with our real estate agents to make the financing process as stress-free as possible," says Amy Hanks, president of Beverly-Hanks Mortgage Services.

Since Beverly-Hanks & Associates introduced Beverly-Hanks Mortgage Services in February 2000, it has grown rapidly. A key factor in the success of the new mortgage company was providing one-stop shopping to real estate clients. With mortgage offices housed under the same roof as the real estate company, clients can literally walk down the hall, become prequalified, write an offer on a new home, and apply for a competitively priced loan without ever leaving the building. In the beginning, Amy was the sole loan officer. The service has been so well received that Beverly-Hanks Mortgage Services has grown to five full-time loan officers in Buncombe, Henderson, and Haywood counties.

Realizing the only constant is change, Beverly-Hanks Mortgage Services continually adds new or improved loan programs. Most any type of financing currently offered in the region can be found here at a competitive rate. A short list of

loan programs would include conventional, jumbo, FHA, VA, most types of low-documentation loans, land and residential lot loans, one-close construction/permanent loans, first-time buyer programs, commercial financing, and more. By taking the guesswork out of financing, the mortgage team can guide clients through the mortgage process, evaluate each client's needs, and help find the customized loan package that matches their unique circumstances. This personalized service has cultivated long-lasting relationships with past clients and has generated new customers who are eager to receive the attention they deserve.

As in the general brokerage business, establishing long-lasting friendships with customers and referral partners is part of the culture. Beverly-Hanks Mortgage Services is dedicated to serving the community on a business level and a personal level. Loan officers are an integral part of the communities in which they live, contributing to a multitude of charitable causes.

For top-notch professional service, competitive rates, a wide range of products, friendly loan officers, and one-stop shopping, Beverly-Hanks Mortgage Services and Beverly-Hanks & Associates offer an easy choice. ❖

▲ Beverly-Hanks Mortgage Services serves the company on a personal level as well, providing support for a number of local riding groups and other charitable organizations.

"We are dedicated to exceeding expectations and working as a team with our real estate agents to make the financing process as stress-free as possible," says Amy Hanks, president of Beverly-Hanks Mortgage Services.

a great place to call home

Asheville's neighborhoods represent the past and present, and always with individualized charm. From stately dwellings on shaded lawns and sprawling waterfront manses, to valley suburbs cloistered off of the Blue Ridge Parkway and quaint abodes that have sheltered several generations, Asheville's neighborhoods are homes because of the warmth of the people who live within them. With the varied attractions of Asheville only minutes away, the residents of these mountain communities are blessed with limitless options for passing the time, whether sharing festivities with friends or, like Jim Kransberger, a locally based sports photographer, relaxing solo on placid Beaver Lake in Lake View Park, one of Asheville's long-established neighborhoods. However, those who prefer the buzz of the city can always choose to relocate to Asheville's old-made-new-again refurbished and trendy downtown lofts.

all photos by rod reilly

A quaint, tree-lined neighborhood offers a delightful way to live, with great

houses, great neighbors, and lifelong friends in a wonderful city atmosphere.

PULLIAM PROPERTIES INC.: the right company in the right city

photo by rod reilly

▲ Meeting with Lance Carter, owner of Southside Café Restaurant. Lance has been a tenant at the Dingle Creek Crossing shopping center for sixteen years.

Rusty Pulliam, president and CEO of Pulliam Properties Inc., can easily pinpoint his company's key to success. "We put the right properties in the right location at the right time," he says of the family-owned, full-service commercial real estate and development firm founded by his father, Winston W. Pulliam. It may sound like a simple strategy, but it actually takes a great deal of market knowledge, ingenuity, and effort to get the formula just right. Fortunately, that's exactly what Pulliam Properties is known for in Asheville.

The Pulliam name is recognizable thanks in large part to Winston Pulliam's vision to develop the south end of Asheville in the late 1960s. He had the foresight to realize that the area between Biltmore Village and the Henderson County line, which featured nothing but vacant, undeveloped terrain along a two-lane road, had great potential. Therefore, he began purchasing parcels of land in the area and held on to them until the time was right to spearhead a large-scale development initiative. By 1982, when he opened his own real estate

(continued on page 126)

photo by rod reilly

▲ Standing in front of a large development parcel that is about to be developed into condominiums and commercial outparcels, Rusty and Winston Pulliam understand that their combined vision will turn this blank slate into a bustling and profitable location for Asheville.

◄ The manager and staff of the Texas Roadhouse Grill Restaurant have every confidence in Rusty Pulliam, who helped the owners of the establishment find the perfect location for the now-popular eatery. And thanks to Rusty's insight, residents from around Asheville can enjoy the delicious food served up here every day of the week.

photo by rod reilly

Today, Pulliam Properties owns more than seventy commercial properties throughout Asheville.

photo by rod reilly

The Pulliam name has become synonymous with the growth and development of Asheville. When local residents pass the company's office building in the Walden Ridge Professional Park, they know that great and exciting work is being done behind those doors on behalf of the city, all under the keen direction of Rusty and Winston Pulliam.

photo by rod reilly

(Pulliam Properties Inc. continued from page 125)

company, Executive Realty, the southernmost region of Asheville was poised to become a burgeoning, bustling commercial district. And accordingly, one of the city's most prolific and influential development organizations sprung into action.

Today, Pulliam Properties owns more than seventy commercial properties throughout Asheville, totaling more than 3.5 million square feet of space. That impressive number continues to grow as the company uses its insight and understanding of the city's growth patterns to help it prosper and thrive. "We were born and raised in Asheville and know the marketplace very well. We've always known what areas of town are going to grow next, and we've been prepared to develop retail, office, or industrial space at the right time," observes Rusty, who began working for the family business in 1986 and took ownership of it in 1993. "But we don't just build to build. We're market driven. We figure out what each area needs, and that's what we develop."

▲ Having a finger on the pulse of Asheville's commercial real estate market has allowed Rusty Pulliam to take the company that his father started and turn it into one of the area's most successful and prolific real estate and development organizations.

Of course, the company is not only responsible for developing and managing the properties it owns, but also for acting as a real estate brokerage firm that places tenants in commercial properties. According to Rusty, "We have helped various types of companies find the sites that are best for them, from restaurants, hotels, doctors' offices, industrial clients, etc., and those businesses have stayed here and prospered very well." They also have benefited from the Pulliams' brokerage and management philosophies, which include everything from listening to clients to figuring out where they need to be located in Asheville to treating tenants and clients the way they themselves would want to be treated. Rusty goes on to say, "We care about our clients, and we want to see them succeed."

Luckily, the father-son duo of Winston Pulliam, who now serves as company chairman, and Rusty Pulliam, who changed the firm's name from Executive Realty to Pulliam Properties in 1999, has created an environment in which companies can succeed. Winston brings to the table his astuteness in land purchasing, while Rusty has elevated the company to a whole new level with his expertise and vision in project development. Pulliam Properties also has seven sales associates and three staff members who strive to uphold Pulliam Properties' outstanding reputation with their exceptional work, and it's no wonder that the company has made such a highly regarded name for itself.

Of course, doing what's best for the community has also served the company well. In addition to a wide variety of community service efforts, from Winston's work with the North Carolina Environmental Management Commission and the Asheville Economic Development Commission to Rusty's involvement on the board of directors for the Asheville Chamber of Commerce, Ralph Sexton Ministries, and the YMCA, the Pulliams and their team have dedicated themselves to being good stewards of the land and the landscape. In fact, in 2002, Rusty Pulliam became the only real estate developer in Western North Carolina to ever receive Quality Forward's Environmental Excellence Award, which is the highest environmental quality award in the region. He has injected that eco-friendly mind-set into Pulliam Properties' newest project: Weirbridge Village, a development of 336 residential condos that will be the largest Gold Level LEEDs-certified green building residential project to date in the United States.

The leap into the residential market is not surprising for the company, which continues to evolve as Asheville does. As Rusty concludes, "We have had a very solid impact on the growth of Asheville over the last thirty years, and it feels great to be able to do that for this city." ❖

▲ Working together has been a great joy for the father-and-son team of Winston and Rusty Pulliam. Here, they take a moment to review site plans for Pulliam Properties' newest mixed-use development in South Asheville, which promises to be as successful as the company's countless other projects.

photo by rod reilly

photo by rod reilly

photo by mario morgado

(left page)

The Victorian boardinghouse memorialized by Thomas Clayton Wolfe in his novel *Look Homeward, Angel* today immortalizes the author whose writing was once praised by critics as superior to that of William Faulkner. In 1929, when the autobiographical novel was published, residents of Asheville considered it scandalous, but the city's citizens soon honored the prolific author who died early at the age of thirty-eight. The Thomas Wolfe Memorial is now a literary landmark open to the public for tours and events throughout the year. "I spent time relaxing on the front porch of the Thomas Wolfe house while attending a friend's wedding," said Tanya Abreu (left), pictured here with Fey Ruback. "I enjoyed Asheville and the beautiful vistas that the home provided."

(right page)

Asheville's downtown has a vibe unlike any other. Lovingly restored and with an eye toward incorporating both the natural and man-made worlds, the area is hip and progressive while also retaining much of its turn-of-the-twentieth-century charm, friendliness, and, most importantly, sense of pride in the community.

photo by rod reilly

BRUISIN' ALES: way beyond ninety-nine bottles of beer on the wall

photo by tim barnwell

▲ Bruisin' Ales' small tasting bar offers the perfect locale for weekly beer tastings. Here, owners Jason and Julie Atallah *(far right)* relish the opportunity to share some of their favorite brews with customers *(left to right)* Jason Martin, Terri Lechner, and Chris Dotson.

What happens when two self-proclaimed "beerlanthropists" decide to bring their love of beer to a city that's known for its own penchant for high-quality brews? Bruisin' Ales, Asheville's first specialty beer store. Featuring more than 450 beers in a quaint and cozy shop on Broadway Street, this distinctive destination offers beer connoisseurs an experience like they've never had before.

"Bruisin' Ales is unique," explains Jason Atallah, who opened the store in late 2006 with his wife, Julie. "It's a place to see beers you've never seen before."

It's just the type of place the Atallahs yearned for themselves when they first discovered a shared love of quality beers while living in Allentown, Pennsylvania. Frequenters of Shangy's, one of the country's largest distributors of domestic and foreign import beers, Jason and Julie didn't take long to find a mentor in Mr. Shangy, who introduced them to "big beers" at an early legal age. Belgians ultimately became the couple's personal favorite.

When Jason and Julie moved to North Carolina and couldn't find the beers they enjoyed, a plan began to brew. "During visits back north, we would skip the airlines and drive eight hours so we could load up on five or more cases. We introduced these beers to friends in the Charlotte area and became the dorky beer snobs," Julie quips. The experience, as well as the state lifting the 6 percent alcohol by volume cap on beer in 2005, encouraged the husband-and-wife team to open their own storefront in Asheville, thanks in part to the town's "intense love for beer."

Today, with eight hundred square feet of space painted red, yellow, and black to match the Belgian flag and twelve hundred square feet of inventory, Bruisin' Ales is a beer enthusiast's dream come true. Patrons will find Belgians, Belgian-style, high-gravity, craft brews, microbrews, and the very best available beers from around the world. The shop also offers an array of supplemental items, such as proper glassware, apparel, books, magazines, and other merchandise.

In addition, beer tastings are weekly events at the store's small tasting bar. That's because the Atallahs' goal is not only to provide the best selection and service in town, but also to educate consumers about beer. "The complexity of beer is so underrated," Julie notes. "You hear so much about wine, and we hope to show that beer is just as complex and interesting."

And because Bruisin' Ales adds to its vast inventory weekly, customers will always find something new on the shelves. This alone makes visiting the store a bona fide event. "We offer more than a beer shopping experience," Jason concludes. "We want Bruisin' Ales to be a true destination for beer lovers." ❖

When Chris Dotson wants to pick out a new beer to try, he knows to head over to Bruisin' Ales, where owner Julie Atallah can take him through Asheville's largest beer selection. Carrying everything from Belgians to microbrews, this destination spot allows beer connoisseurs the chance to browse through more than 450 beers in a warm and welcoming environment.

photo by tim barnwell

When Jason and Julie moved to North Carolina and couldn't find the beers they enjoyed, a plan began to brew.

all photos by rod reilly

(left page)

The city of Asheville excels at reclaiming its wonderful old buildings. Opened in 1929, the Grove Arcade thrived until World War II as one of the country's leading public markets. Renovated into the Grove Arcade Arts and Heritage Gallery, it features the crafts, music, and stories of the Blue Ridge. Other refurbished downtown buildings include the 1926 Flat Iron Building. Marked by Asheville artist Reed Todd's sculptural homage, it now houses sought-after retail and residential space.

(right page)

In a place as attractive and temperate as Asheville, folks try to do as much as possible outdoors. In the city itself, downtown is the locus for urban adventuring. The city is filled with dozens of spots to enjoy an al fresco repast, from casual coffee shops to fine dining venues, as well as indoor entertainment at various bookstores, specialty shops, and art galleries. A Far Away Place is a great spot to find sacred art, masks, textiles, jewelry, and instruments from throughout India, Asia, and Africa.

CAROLINA DAY SCHOOL: discover the promise, inspire the journey, celebrate the achievement

photo by thomas s. england

▲ Middle School teacher Chris McGrath leads a lively discussion in his single-gender language arts class. After much study of the latest brain development research, Carolina Day School began to offer its students the option of single-gender classes at the sixth- and seventh-grade levels as a way to more fully meet their individual learning needs.

Responsibility. Thirst for personal excellence. Achievement. Compassion. All desirable values, but they cannot be acquired in a vacuum. They have to be taught. Since its establishment, Carolina Day School has embodied those values as operating tenets, challenging its students to grow in mind, body, heart, and human spirit.

"We emphasized character education long before it was a buzzword," says Head of School Bev Sgro. "Students learn the meaning of our four tenets from the beginning. They are part of our curriculum, part of how we all live our lives."

Established in 1987 as a comprehensive independent school through the merger of Asheville Country Day School and St. Genevieve/Gibbons Hall, Carolina Day School consists of four divisions: Lower School (prekindergarten through fifth grade),

Key School (for bright students first through eighth grade with language-based learning differences), Middle School (sixth through eighth grade), and Upper School (ninth through twelfth grade).

Accredited by the Southern Association of Independent Schools and the Southern Association of Colleges and Schools, Carolina Day School boasts rigorous academic programs at all levels, including a college preparatory program featuring eighteen advanced placement courses in the Upper School. Add to that an impressive arts program, a modern language program (including thirteen years of Spanish and seven years of French), sixteen different sports, community service initiatives both inside and out of the classroom, and the result is a remarkable record of student achievement.

(continued on page 136)

▲ Upper School sophomores complete a chemistry lab assignment. As a college preparatory school, Carolina Day School features a rigorous, broad-based curriculum with many AP courses and small classes. The school is also committed through its community service programs and Honor Code to helping students achieve success beyond college and career and into the rest of their lives.

photo by thomas s. england

photo by thomas s. england

◀ Learning starts early for these Lower School students, who begin their educational journeys in a safe and stimulating environment. In addition to regular classroom instruction, students are provided opportunities to work with their hands, play games, write stories, and perform science experiments. They are even given public speaking projects.

"We emphasized character education long before it was a buzzword," says Head of School Bev Sgro.

(Carolina Day School continued from page 135)

photo by thomas s. england

▲ The full- and part-day programs offered at Carolina Day's Key School are geared toward bright students in first through eighth grades with language-based learning differences. Speaking in front of a group and learning to listen attentively are just two of the many ways in which students learn to overcome their challenges and reach their maximum potential.

With a median SAT score averaging 200 points higher than the state scores and 150 points higher than national scores, virtually 100 percent of Carolina Day School seniors attend college, and every year the school has several students recognized by the National Merit Scholarship Corporation.

What accounts for such success? With 100 faculty members and 650 students, small classes certainly play a part. Says Admissions Director Robin Goertz, whose daughter currently attends the school, "Carolina Day is large enough to be stimulating and diverse, but small enough that the teachers know all the students and work with them individually."

Promoting a transformational culture that seeks change and growth, the school provides plenty of ongoing educational opportunities for faculty as well, many of whom hold advanced degrees in their subject matter. As for instruction itself, the school believes that the best way to teach is to inspire.

"We motivate by example, not pressure," continues Sgro. "We are very clear about our expectations, and we provide the resources for students to meet them."

The goal of each of the school's four divisions is not only to teach students at their developmental level, but also to impart the skills required to move on to the next. Teachers in all divisions write their own customized curriculum, utilizing interdisciplinary techniques and incorporating the latest in brain and learning research.

For instance, because young children learn best by doing, computer usage is not part of the curriculum until the third grade. Likewise, in response to the latest research in gender-based learning differences at the middle school level, Carolina Day School offers gender-separated sixth-and seventh-grade classes to allow boys and girls to reach their full potential in a relaxed and nonjudgmental environment.

"One of the biggest challenges in education is understanding what children need," says Sgro. "How do we respond to fads? We don't. We have the luxury as an independent school of doing our research and making deliberate decisions."

The school's commitment to critical thinking naturally passes down to the students. "It's pervasive in everything they do," says Goertz of her daughter's education. "Teaching students to discover and apply their abilities is what Carolina Day School does best." ❖

The Orange Peel Social Aid & Pleasure Club of Asheville bills itself as our nation's premiere live music hall and concert venue. And if you don't believe it, check this out: such noted acts as Bob Dylan, Ben Harper, Blondie, Sonic Youth, Steel Pulse, and the Smashing Pumpkins regularly grace their stage—as do a variety of up-and-coming local and regional acts. On this particular night, local-band-done-good Toubab Krewe had everyone dancing to their unique brand of self-styled "afro-cowboy-ninja-surf music." Good thing the Orange Peel is also known for its several-hundred-square-foot dance floor . . .

festivals and fun

An abundance of festivals and events in and around Asheville provide opportunities to celebrate the area's Appalachian heritage. From craft demonstrations and storytelling to mountain music and dance to food and games, the area's festivals recall the legacy of the people who have lived and worked in these mountains for generations. Colorful and eclectic, Asheville's festivals fill the calendar year-round and offer something for every member of the family to enjoy. With the weather in this region especially inviting, spending time outdoors is an element central to life in these parts. As a result, many festivals include an outdoor recreation component as well. Whether it is horseback riding, a carriage ride, or a hike along a mountain trail, festivalgoers who want to spend time in the fresh air have plenty of options for taking part in the simple pleasures that make this area unique.

all photos by rod reilly

GROVE PARK INN: enter a world where history meets luxury

▲ Enjoy breathtaking views as you dine on the Sunset Terrace at the Grove Park Inn Resort and Spa.

photo by rod reilly

Combining the elegance of a bygone era with the best in modern treatments and amenities, the Grove Park Inn Resort & Spa is renowned as a world-class leisure destination. Built in 1913 of local bedrock by pharmaceutical entrepreneur Edwin Wiley Grove in the tradition of the grand mountain lodges of the American West, the Grove Park Inn has over the years attracted such distinguished guests as F. Scott Fitzgerald, Ralph Waldo Emerson, Eleanor Roosevelt, and no fewer than eight presidents.

Over a century later, the resort continues its legacy of warm, attentive, legendary service, offering guests a myriad of ways in which to relax and rejuvenate. Situated on 161 acres in the Blue Ridge foothills overlooking Asheville, the resort's complex comprises the original Main Inn with two modern wings, four award-winning restaurants, a charming guest cottage, a championship Donald Ross par-70 golf course, and a full-service sports complex.

The Grove Park Inn is also distinguished by its state-of-the-art, forty-thousand-square-foot Spa, which is built partially underground. Completed as part of a $42 million renovation begun in 1998, the Spa not only offers a variety of restorative treatments, including a line of signature treatments called the "Heaven Series," but also a 120-degree eucalyptus steam room, therapeutic waterfall pools, outdoor heated pool, and plenty of indoor and outdoor space for quiet contemplation.

Still going strong nearly a century after its establishment, the Grove Park Inn is an Asheville landmark. It has also earned accolades as a top-ten spa worldwide from such esteemed industry publications as *Fodor's*, *Travel & Leisure*, and *Spa.com* for providing guests with its unequalled blend of history, style, and service. ❖

Still going strong nearly a century after its establishment, the Grove Park Inn is an Asheville landmark.

It bills itself as the "Front Porch of Western North Carolina." That's because the small town of Black Mountain, located a half hour northeast of Asheville, is about as friendly and laid back as it gets. Its charming shops, restaurants, and galleries, coupled with its bucolic mountain setting, make it a popular and relaxing destination.

MOUNTAIN AIR COUNTRY CLUB — the sky's the limit

▲ Mountain Air Country Club's championship eighteen-hole golf course is one of the major attractions of this outstanding community. Just like the view from every green and tee box, the vistas golfers enjoy while playing Austin Mountain's celebrated Hole No. 1 is as awe-inspiring as the shot is challenging.

I magine waking up early in the morning, sitting down at the breakfast table with a hot cup of coffee, and looking out across your own backyard to watch the sun slowly rise over the majestic peaks of the Blue Ridge Mountains. That peaceful, awe-inspiring experience is possible every day at Mountain Air Country Club, a thirteen-hundred-acre private mountaintop residential community located just thirty-five minutes northeast of Asheville in Burnsville, North Carolina. Sitting at 4,919 feet in elevation and surrounded by a 2,000-foot-deep valley, Mountain Air is virtually heaven on earth, enveloping residents in Mother Nature's splendor throughout the year while giving them a true sense of home.

The award-winning golf community, which has been honored for its magnificent and varied single-family homes by the National Association of Home Builders, is the brainchild of Burnsville's very own Banks and Young families, who own the thirteen hundred acres behind the gates. Their idea was to create a community that not only provided beautiful homesites and elegant homes amidst some of the Blue Ridge Mountains' most breathtaking and challenging terrain, but also a place

(continued on page 144)

▲ Located a convenient thirty-five-minute drive northeast of Asheville, North Carolina, Mountain Air Country Club residents enjoy the pinnacle of Mountaintop living with edge-of-the-world views.

◀ At Mountain Air County Club, getting back to nature is as simple as walking out on the back deck. And each terrace not only offers an excellent place to spend an evening communing with Mother Nature herself, among stately trees offset by splendid mountain panoramas, but also a setting for both relaxing and entertaining.

photo by scott indermaur

Mountain Air is virtually heaven on earth, enveloping residents in Mother Nature's splendor.

(Mountain Air Country Club, continued from page 143)

where residents could enjoy a feeling of community and revel in an array of unparalleled amenities. Through thoughtful development and an unwavering dedication to environmental stewardship, the local families made their vision a reality.

Today, Mountain Air Country Club features home-sites that range from $400,000 to more than $2 million, condominium homes from $399,000 to more than $4 million, and custom homes from $650,000 to more than $5 million. Potential residents can easily find the home style that meets their personality, thanks to the fact that the community offers several distinct neighborhoods within its gates, including such locales as the Cabins at Creekside, Hawks Ledge Cottages, Spring Rock, Timber Sky, and Waterfall Cabins, as well as Mountain Air's newest addition, Settlers Edge. This neighborhood, which is nestled at nearly 4,500 feet along the edge of a mountainside, overlooks the Black Mountain range and Mount Mitchell, recognized as the highest point in the eastern United States, and is bordered by the community's paved private runway. It will boast eleven original estate homes by Al Platt, the HGTV 2006 Dream Home Architect, among other home ownership opportunities.

Homesites and homes like these are a hallmark of Mountain Air, as is the community's championship eighteen-hole golf course—one of its most prominent and celebrated amenities. The course, which includes a signature cliff-side 8th hole that looks east across a valley to the peak of Mount Mitchell, drops 900 feet of elevation as golfers traverse its tee boxes and greens. And from the front nine to the back nine, the fifty- to one-hundred-mile views provide a spectacular backdrop to any day out on the course.

photo by scott indermaur

▲ The homes found in the Hawks Ledge Cottages neighborhood give homeowners a real feel for mountain living. In addition to amazing views of the surrounding peaks and charming cabinlike architecture, the upscale residences are warm and cozy, with interiors that evoke a true sense of rustic elegance.

Of course, Mountain Air also offers a plethora of additional amenities, from tennis courts and a swimming pool to a popular community clubhouse—all with the same picturesque vistas that can be enjoyed from anywhere in the community. Furthermore, with the preservation of a one-hundred-acre old-growth forest and creative recreational family programs offered by an in-house naturalist and a director of family recreation, residents of all ages have the chance to explore and become educated about the wondrous world around them. The community's interpretive nature and hiking trails are a great place to start, especially during the summer months, when Mountain Air's always-pleasant temperatures rarely reach into the eighties.

And while the community's seemingly removed setting allows residents to escape the hustle and bustle of city living,

its easy access to charming Burnsville, only five minutes away, and lively Asheville, a mere thirty-five-minute drive, gives them the chance to take advantage of North Carolina's finest whenever they please. With dining, shopping, the arts, and culture abounding just down the road, Mountain Air truly offers the best of all possible worlds. In fact, the community's extensive list of attributes makes it an ideal locale for everyone, from primary homeowners to second-home residents. It's for those who want to feel at one with nature and those who admire and respect outstanding mountain-inspired architecture. It's for families who enjoy being on the go and those who prefer a quiet Sunday at home. Most importantly, it's for those who want more than a house—those who want a place to call home. ❖

Mountain Air Country Club's younger residents can always find something interesting to do. With interpretive nature and hiking trails, as well as a resident naturalist on site, the community offers little ones the perfect opportunity to explore the incredible world around them. And whether it's a hike or a Salamander Safari (pictured here), the adventure promises to be as educational as it is entertaining.

There really is something for everyone at Mountain Air Country Club. In fact, the Mountain Market at the Village Green stocks everything from pantry staples to fine wine to freshly prepared deli sandwiches. And thanks to its convenient location, the market makes a quick trip to the store a piece of cake.

hat a wonderful way to enjoy the beauty of the fall. The crisp air

all photos by rod reilly

(far left)

Asheville lives at the top of the list of places to enjoy all things autumn. When the distinctive scent of fall lingers in the fresh mountain air, and temperatures tell us it's time to don our favorite light sweater, we know the kaleidoscope of the season's colors is arriving soon. Take a walk or a jog on one of the trails around the Grove Park Inn. Whether on foot or wheels, there are countless ways to experience fall in Asheville.

(center)

Inspired by the embrace of the trees, David and Carol Swanson enjoy a romantic stroll through one of their favorite neighborhoods. The Swansons, who live in Flat Rock, are typical of the residents of Western North Carolina: they take advantage of the area's pleasant climate and resulting sensational seasons. In addition to the exercise they get from maintaining their two-acre homestead, they often sneak in a walk before dining out, as they did today. To celebrate their forty-first wedding anniversary, the Swansons headed to the Grove Park Inn, arriving early enough to take in the fall colors as an appetizer.

(left)

Whether on foot or on horseback, there are countless ways to experience fall in Asheville. The area boasts many types of trails for walking, jogging, biking, or hiking— or hop in the car and drive the beautiful Blue Ridge Parkway. 'Tis also the season to pop into a local farmers market, or one of the many arts and crafts shows.

and colorful foliage lift the human spirit to new heights.

THE ALPHA GROUP — the local ad agency with global expertise

photo by mario morgado

▲ Jack Becker, senior copywriter, skillfully crafts just the right words for delivering each client's unique message in a memorable way.

Many people know Asheville, North Carolina, as a mountainous getaway replete with rest and recreational options. However, they are probably unaware that Asheville is also a growing city chosen for its quality of life by some of the world's top advertising professionals, who now manage the largest ad agency in the region—The Alpha Group. "I've worked in big agencies around the globe, and we offer every single thing that they can," said Neil Gurney, vice president creative/brand strategy. But The Alpha Group offers something more: personalized service with top-notch expertise, for every client.

"Because of our current clientele, some business owners might think they can't afford The Alpha Group, or that they might be treated as small fish. That's just not the way we work. We give all our clients the same amount of dedication regardless of their budgets," said Brian Hutzler, president.

That dedication means developing exceptional advertisements driven by decades of experience. "We determine how best to utilize every client's investment to reach their audience in the most constructive way. Our job as brand stewards is to make sure that advertising is consistent, relevant, impactful, and it breaks through the clutter," said Hutzler. Breaking through to the right audience, with the right message, via the perfect media combination, The Alpha Group creative team works one-on-one with each customer to create logos, Web sites, brochures, collaterals, or full marketing campaigns. "We're not a big show-and-tell operation where we ask to be left alone for several weeks and then surprise the customer. The creative process is ongoing and always involves the client," explained Gurney.

Involvement includes a "branding cue sort" during which clients participate to determine the tone, image, and message that they hope to deliver. "Your brand lives in someone's head," said Gurney. "We discover why people use your services and what differentiates you from your competitors. We see branding as tapping into the head of the consumer."

Using the best research software available, the firm discovers each client's specific audience and appeals to that audience's emotional triggers concerning an experience or a product. Whether through print, radio, television, direct mail, the Internet, and/or the growing number of new outlets, such as iPod messaging and videos, the company's creative studio, media planning and buying, account service, and production departments satisfy (with significant return on investment) such premiere customers as The Grove Park Inn, Biltmore Farms Inc., Ingle's Supermarkets, Beverly-Hanks and Associates, Southcliff, and WMIT-FM (Billy Graham's Christian radio station).

While the average client/ad agency relationship lasts about three years, The Alpha Group breaks the norm with average client tenure of seven-plus years. "No matter the size of the client, our results are way beyond what they could achieve for themselves, because we use the right media in the right place, and we spend 100 percent of our day making their advertising work for them," said Gurney.

Fun is an essential element of the workday at The Alpha Group. Bridget Risdon, account executive, clearly enjoys discussing a branding strategy with the creative team.

photo by mario morgado

"We determine how best to utilize every client's investment to reach their audience in the most constructive way."

photo by tim barnwell

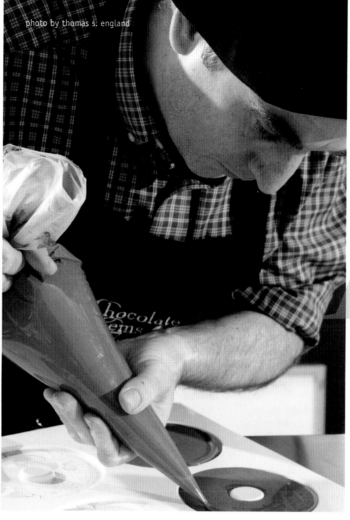

the faces of art in the mountains

Art has a unique sound in the mountains. It's the symphony created by mingling the sound of Jerry Read Smith playing chords on his handcrafted hammer dulcimers with the counterpoint *ping, ping, ping* of Don Howachyn's hammer as he fashions sculptures out of iron, then adding the rich sounds of Pearl Muller's guitar, and topping it off with the heartfelt *oooohs* and *aaaahs* of customers as they watch Andrew Chisholm create Chocolate Gems from the finest American and European ingredients. Whether making instruments, playing music, creating art, or feeding the soul with chocolate, these artists all contribute their unique talents to the richness and culture of Asheville and Black Mountain.

One reason the arts scene in the Asheville area is so vibrant is the conscious effort the community puts forth to attract, encourage, train, showcase, and nurture artists in all fields. With an eye to the practical aspects of being an artist, various scholarships, grants, and awards offer much-needed financial aid. Founded more than forty years ago, the mission of the Asheville Area Arts Council (AAAC) is "to enrich our community by educating all people in the Asheville area about the arts, advocating integration of the arts in all aspects of community life, and supporting artists and arts organization." So far the plan is working just fine.

PLI: unlocking the door to promotional possibilities

photo by alan s. weiner

▲ PLI supplies products for more than fifteen thousand hotels throughout the world. In addition to key cards, PLI also produces gift cards, POS cards, membership and loyalty cards, door hangers, and key card envelopes.

In thousands of hotels around the world, whenever a room door is opened, chances are it was done with a product produced in Asheville. Key cards, now a staple of the hotel industry, are created by one of Asheville's homegrown companies, Plasticard Locktech International (PLI).

Started in the late 1980s by a retiree in his home basement, PLI now employs over 120 people and operates out of a building of more than fifty-four thousand square feet. The company produces in excess of 150 million key cards on an annual basis, each adhering to a PLI standard of quality on which the company was founded.

In fact, delivering consistent quality is one reason for the company's phenomenal growth and for its earning the Asheville Area Chamber of Commerce Sky High Growth Award for eight years. Another element contributing to PLI's expanding operations is its dedication to client satisfaction and ability to consistently exceed customer expectations, a factor recognized in 2005 by the Chamber's Manufacturing Leadership Award. And the company's progress over time stems from its innovation and responsiveness to industry changes, noted by the Chamber in 2007 with an Out on a Limb award.

(continued on page 154)

▲ PLI continuously upgrades equipment to maintain state-of-the-art technology. Manufacturing over 150 million key cards per year, PLI is the nation's largest hotel key card manufacturer.

◀ PLI offers a full-service prepress department, including graphic design, layout, and online proofing. Quality control is a top priority, so PLI conducts quality-control checks during every phase of production.

The company's progress over time stems from its innovation and responsiveness to industry changes.

(PLI, continued from page 153)

As the nation's largest manufacturer of plastic key cards, PLI supplies product for more than fifteen thousand hotels throughout the world. Its impressive client list reads like a directory of hospitality industry giants: Starwood, Hyatt, Marriott, Choice, and Intercontinental Hotel Group all count on PLI for their room keys. For these clients, whose properties include names like Sheraton, Westin, Four Points, Hyatt, Holiday Inn, Residence Inn, Courtyard, Comfort Inn, Clarion, Quality Inn, and more, PLI maintains a stock of more than 12 million key cards and envelopes printed with each hotel's logo.

Beyond essentials imprinted with hotel logos, key cards over time have become much more than just a tool for opening doors. Today, demand is rising for key cards as a medium for advertising, used often by restaurants, banks, theme parks and attractions, family entertainment centers, insurance companies, vacation resorts, and cellular companies.

For example, for Domino's Pizza, PLI produces more than 20 million key cards each year that are placed in nearly 6,000 hotels nationwide and contain the phone number of the nearest restaurant. For Ron Jon Surf Shop, PLI produces thousands of cards and envelopes for placement in Florida hotels, each containing a discount for a nearby store and a bar code to track sales.

Key cards are also fast becoming treasured mementos for a whole range of occasions, from annual meetings and conventions to special festivals and weddings. Much like trading cards, key cards can be customized to contain any message, photo, or graphic element. For instance, PLI created a set of four *Star Wars* key cards for a comic book trade show, which immediately became collectibles to be traded

photo by alan s. weiner

▲ PLI maintains an inventory of over 12 million hotel key cards and envelopes, allowing them to ship most orders within twenty-four hours. PLI processes an average of 275 shipments each day.

and sold. To promote the DreamWorks movie *Madagascar* in its premiering cities, PLI created 1 million special cards and placed them in more than 250 hotels in twelve cities. PLI cards have also been created for conferences and conventions held by Lowe's, Ford, the American Kennel Club, the National Association of Home Builders, UPS, Bank of America, AFLAC, Verizon, and Turner Sports.

In fact, PLI produces more than a half million key cards each year for sports events, venues, and teams. When NASCAR teamed up with Home Depot for a Brickyard race, Tony Stewart was featured on over twenty-eight thousand key cards with bar codes that were placed in 63 hotels in the Indianapolis area. The card also served as a gift card to Home Depot, but guests had to bring the card into a Home Depot store to discover the value of the card, which ranged from five dollars to five hundred dollars. PLI has also produced cards for NCAA Basketball, World Wrestling Entertainment, the National Basketball Association, Major League Baseball, NFL teams, the Super Bowl, and numerous bowl games, including the Orange, Cotton, Fiesta, Independence, and Outback bowls.

In addition to key cards, PLI's hotel product lineup includes items such as key card envelopes, door hangers, cleaning cards, channel guides, and presentation folders. PLI also manufactures gift cards, loyalty cards, membership cards, luggage tags, key fobs, and credential and parking passes.

Although they may be small, PLI's products are making a big impact around the world. ❖

photo by alan s. weiner

PLI has the best customer service in the industry. From advertising programs and event key cards to hotel sales and customer service, PLI assists a variety of customers through every step of the process.

photo by alan s. weiner

PLI houses a six-color press, the largest printing press in Western North Carolina. In addition, PLI has five- and two-color presses, as well as other finishing equipment, allowing PLI to print virtually any product on paper or plastic.

asheville's crafty engineer

When John E. Cram opened New Morning Gallery in Historic Biltmore Village in 1972, he did so in a sleepy little mountain town that didn't even have a highway yet. But that's not what he saw when he looked at the city he had chosen to call home after relocating to the South. "Asheville was a phoenix rising from the ashes," he notes, referring to the town's tenacious efforts to pay off its Depression-era debts and return to its boomtown status. "Its potential was phenomenal." So with a five-hundred-dollar investment and a keen business sense, Cram turned his love of the visual arts and crafts into a venture that would one day bring a bona fide renaissance to downtown Asheville.

New Morning Gallery, an "Art for Living craft gallery" that showcases decorative and functional handcrafted pieces, was the perfect fit for a city with a history steeped in the crafts industry. Over the years, the gallery has attracted locals and tourists from around the country, turning Asheville into a destination spot for craft enthusiasts. Its success inspired Cram to take a risk with a building he had purchased in the downtown area. In 1991, he opened Blue Spiral 1, a contemporary fine art gallery that presents the works of southeastern artists and serves as the home of the estate of twentieth-century modernist Will Henry Stevens. Even before the stylish space was done being converted, other local entrepreneurs recognized its promise—thanks in large part to Cram's reputation—and wanted to locate their own businesses near it. The presence of Blue Spiral 1 drew restaurateurs, coffee shop owners, music club proprietors, bookstore owners, and many others. Today, downtown Asheville, which is often called the Santa Fe of the East, is a thriving center of cultural activity. And with Cram's ever-growing enterprise, including the openings of Bellagio Art-to-Wear, the Fine Arts Theatre, Bellagio Everyday, and Kenilworth Gardens, Asheville continues to enjoy a lively and burgeoning arts scene.

In recent years, Cram's affection for Asheville's history, culture, and people has encouraged him to unite with his neighbors and fellow business owners to help preserve the city. The reason is simple. "The people here get it," he reveals. "And as Margaret Mead said, 'Never doubt that a small group of thoughtful, committed people can change the world.'" In Asheville, John E. Cram is living proof of that.

John E. Cram
Art Gallery Owner

Continuing to breathe life into Asheville's flourishing arts scene.

photo by tim barnwell

Asheville has always had a reputation as a health retreat. As far back as 1795, people came to heal themselves here. Today's residents take a more proactive approach, one that emphasizes healthy living and exercise. David Wiggins, of the accounting firm Dixon Hughes, leads his fellow coworkers Amy Bibby, James Baley, Tina Spring, and Michael Rauchwarg on an early-morning run through the North Carolina Arboretum.

Downtown Asheville is an interesting collection of restaurants, shops, galleries, museums, intriguing architecture, and more. One of the best ways to soak up the flavor of any city is on foot, but Moving Sidewalk Tours makes the experience even better. Gliding along on a Segway, visitors get a unique view of downtown without having to walk a single step.

photo by scott indermaur

photo by tim barnwell

photo by rod reilly

The Vance pioneer homestead was built in 1795 by David Vance I, one of five in a line of courageous family members—including North Carolina governor and U.S. senator Zebulon Baird Vance—who dedicated their lives to public service. Situated in a valley sheltered by the Blue Ridge Mountains, the property has been restored and serves as an interpretive center and site for year-round special events.

SOUTHERN COMMUNITY BANK AND TRUST: familiar faces abound

(Left to right) Dan Anderson, Leisa Capps, Jason Chambers, Christine Burrell, Charles Frederick, Brad Blackburn . . . "Small Enough to Care."

photo by tim barnwell

When Southern Community Bank and Trust entered the Asheville market in early 2007, it was the newest full-service financial institution in town. No one would have known that, though, because the entire staff was made up of longtime local residents who had strong ties to the community. And that's exactly how it remains today.

"We wanted to create a hometown-bank feel," explains Charles Frederick, western regional president. "Our goal is to provide sophisticated products and services equivalent to those at big banks, but in a small, service-oriented environment."

Undoubtedly, Southern Community Bank and Trust, founded in Winston-Salem in 1996 and recognized as one of North Carolina's fastest-growing banks with $1.5 billion in assets, has accomplished its mission. The institution offers everything from personal checking and online banking to a full suite of business and investor products and services, including remote deposit capture and a deposit courier for customer convenience. In fact, the business sector is a focal point in the Asheville marketplace, where the bank specializes in meeting the financial needs of small businesses, residential real estate and construction companies, and emerging professionals.

Also for convenience, Southern Community Bank and Trust plans to add more branches in the area over the short term. "We have a consistent vision of being a long-term, growth-oriented institution, but we're still 'small enough to care,'" Frederick says. "And we're changing the way people feel about banking." ❖

"We have a consistent vision of being a long-term, growth-oriented institution, but we're still 'small enough to care.'"

(left)

Location, location, location: It's what makes the Asheville Renaissance Hotel a favorite with so many travelers to the city. Centrally situated and within walking distance of downtown, the hotel is also minutes away from the Asheville Civic Center, the Asheville Regional Airport, Biltmore Estate, and the Blue Ridge Parkway.

(below)

Everything about Biltmore is done on a grand scale. The French Renaissance chateau is modeled after the great French chateaux on the Loire Valley. The palatial home, built by George Washington Vanderbilt, has 250 rooms, an indoor pool, and a bowling alley, and is surrounded by acres and acres of grounds designed by Frederick Law Olmsted, the father of landscape architecture.

ASHEVILLE VEIN CENTER & MEDICAL SPA: helping you look and feel great at any age

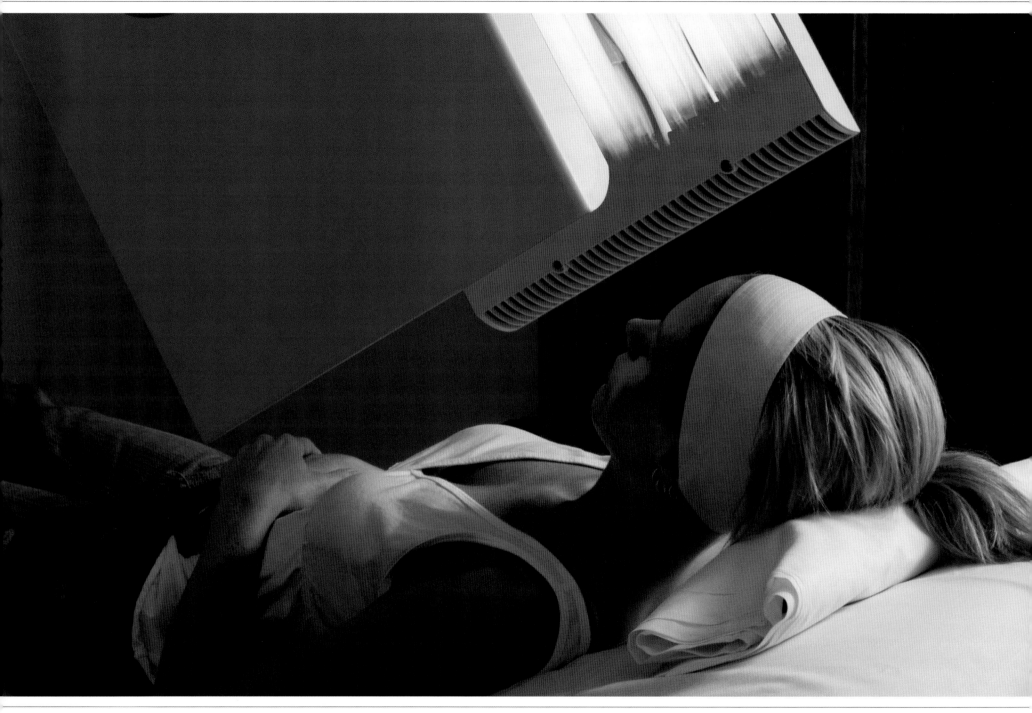

photo by tim barnwell

▲ Acne sufferers often notice visible and long-lasting relief after only one treatment with a revolutionary photodynamic Blue Light Therapy treatment offered at the Asheville Vein Center & Medical Spa. The safe and painless blue light exposure kills the bacteria that causes acne and clogged pores and reduces pore size.

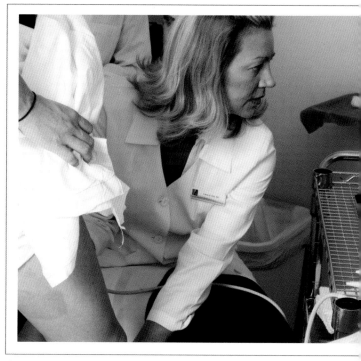

The physicians and staff at Asheville Vein Center & Medical Spa are as passionate about patient education and satisfaction as they are about staying on top of the latest techniques in vein therapy, skin rejuvenation, and antiaging procedures. "We believe informed patients make better decisions and know when they are getting the finest possible care," says surgeon and founder Dr. Laura Ellis.

Perhaps it is this philosophy—along with the physicians' experience and expertise—that makes the center one of the region's most sought-after medical spas, as well as one of the leading vein centers in the country.

Dr. Ellis is a founding member of Vein Affiliates, a national organization of surgical specialists with expertise in venous surgery, and has published major articles on laser skin rejuvenation. Dr. Allan Huffman, a vascular surgeon specializing in minimally invasive laser surgery for varicose veins and spider vein treatments, is a member of Vein Affiliates and a Fellow of the American College of Surgeons.

Asheville Vein Center & Medical Spa serves as a preferred training center for surgeons from all over the United States who are interested in learning leading-edge laser techniques and vein treatments.

"Varicose and spider veins are very common," Dr. Ellis explains, "and cause a variety of symptoms in both men and women. It is estimated that almost half of women aged forty to fifty are affected, and this percentage increases with age."

(continued on page 164)

photo by tim barnwell

▲ Most people don't realize that varicose vein disease is largely an inherited malady that can now be treated, and usually cured without painful surgery. Here, Dr. Laura Ellis performs an ultrasound exam to determine the severity of a patient's venous insufficiency. Such examinations are part of a complete consultation performed at the Asheville Vein Center & Medical Spa.

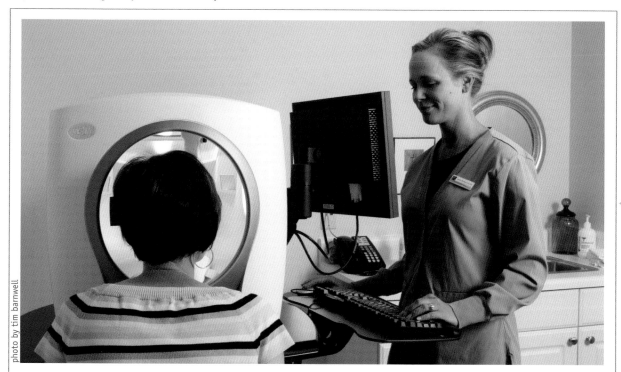

photo by tim barnwell

◄ Carmen Blackwell, RN, performs a VISIA Skin Analysis on the patient. The computerized technology provides measurable values for six areas of complexion health including wrinkles, sun damage, evenness, and enlarged pores. Patients receive visual reports (reflecting progress over time) accompanied by rejuvenation treatments and ongoing skin-care methods. VISIA is an integral part of the many top-notch skin health and anti-aging specialties offered at the center.

"We believe informed patients make better decisions and know when they are getting the finest possible care."

(Asheville Vein Center continued from page 163)

But Drs. Ellis and Huffman don't just treat this unsightly and often painful condition, they can actually cure it, thanks to the new, minimally invasive technique of laser ablation. This virtually painless procedure consists of cauterizing dysfunctional veins—most commonly the great saphenous vein—using a small laser fiber inserted into the leg through an IV.

"Laser ablation is overwhelmingly successful," says Dr. Huffman. "A full 98 percent of patients are effectively cured. Even in the rare cases of recurrence, treatment with this new laser technique is manageable and highly effective."

Best of all, the treatment is performed in a comfortable office setting under only local anesthesia. Patients walk out of the office afterward and resume normal activities in a couple of days. Unlike the outdated "vein-stripping" procedures, laser treatment eliminates the need for large incisions, requires no stitches, and leaves no unsightly scars.

Soon after the Asheville Vein Center opened in 2004, satisfied patients began urging the doctors to offer a variety of antiaging treatments.

The center now offers a full array of medical spa treatments—minimally invasive preventative and corrective procedures designed to improve skin health and appearance— including BOTOX® Cosmetic and Restylane wrinkle reduction, IPL age spot removal, mesotherapy fat reduction, Sculptra® and Radiesse® facial contouring, laser peel and microdermabrasion skin rejuvenation, photodynamic therapy for precancerous skin conditions, blue light therapy for acne treatment, and permanent laser hair removal.

All med spa treatments begin with a detailed computerized VISIA skin analysis of six factors of skin health, including pigmentation, pores, and evenness. Patients then receive a customized report with personal treatment and skin-care recommendations.

Asheville Vein Center & Medical Spa is the only center in Western North Carolina to offer med spa treatments under the care of surgical specialists, and the only clinic in the Southeast to offer the new Web-based Aesthetic Imaging service, which gives patients the ability to view and share their treatment results at any time from the privacy of their own homes.

State-of-the art technology, with personal attention and expert care, provided by leading surgical specialists—that's the prescription Asheville Vein Center & Medical Spa follows to help people look and feel their best. ❖

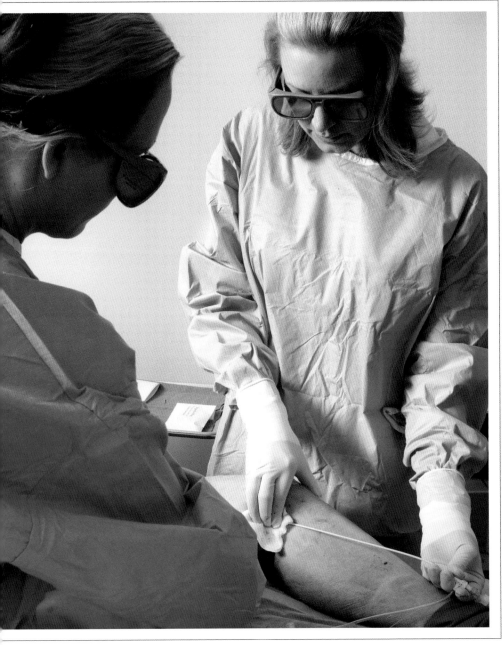

photo by tim barnwell

▲ "People don't have to live with the achey, swollen legs of venous disease," says Dr. Laura Ellis, shown here with Carmen Blackwell, RN, performing laser surgery for varicose veins. The progressive procedures performed at the Asheville Vein Center & Medical Spa can eliminate such problems immediately and permanently. Patients can return to their normal routines after two days of rest, much happier and pain free.

photo by rod reilly

photo by rod reilly

(above)

Many people know of Joe Kimmel's love of art and his many philanthropic gifts to the Asheville community. However, not generally known is that he not only appreciates and collects art, he creates it as well. Some of his designs are on sale at J. Kimmel Fine Jewelry, which is located on the ground floor of his company's building on Page Avenue downtown.

(right)

Judging from the sign, this building in downtown Asheville is home to Pearlman's Super Furniture Store. Right? Wrong. It was their original location, but no more. In 1991, Joe Kimmel, owner of Kimmel & Associates Inc., bought the art-deco building and had it restored. Kimmel & Associates, the largest executive search firm in the nation specializing in the construction industry, now occupies the building, but unless you know where to look, you'll never find the entrance, and that suits Joe Kimmel's sense of humor just fine.

CAROLINA FIRST BANK: "we take your banking personally!"

photo by tim barnwell

▲ Construction begins on Carolina First's new corporate headquarters in downtown Asheville. Carolina First is a "super community" bank that can make financial decisions locally as a hometown organization while having the big-bank capacity to stimulate commerce and fund multimillion-dollar projects.

sheville has a charm, almost a mystique unlike any other town or city in Western North Carolina. It is the crown jewel of this region—our closest claim to cosmopolitan. Therein lies its mystique or incongruence. Asheville is really an overgrown macrocosm of most other Western North Carolina towns, except that it has a diversity, vibrancy, and uniqueness that provides a culture and quality of life comparable to any major city in the United States," said J. W. Davis, president of Carolina First.

Carolina First Bank is a subsidiary of the South Financial Group, a holding company for which Davis also serves on the corporate board of directors. You might say that banking is in his blood. In 1997, Davis founded and opened MountainBank in Hendersonville, North Carolina, serving as president and chief executive officer there until 2003. At that time, MountainBank partnered with Carolina First Bank and, by virtue of the merger, became part of the Carolina First Bank's three-state franchise. Acting on a commitment to expand the franchise within the

(continued on page 168)

Carmen Kniesly, like all Carolina First employees, knows that exceptional customer service is key to the bank's mission.

photo by tim barnwell

photo by tim barnwell

Carolina First's Shawn Fitzpatrick (left), senior vice president, and Scott Frierson, executive vice president, diligently adhere to the bank's core values of integrity, professionalism, relationships, balance, and passion for serving customers without the impediments of big-bank bureaucracy.

"Banking is not a commodity business. It's really not about money or finance; it's about humanity."

Parker Spears, manager of Carolina First's Merrimon Avenue Branch, helps a customer open a new account. Putting customers first with flexible and responsive service is the organization's guiding principle. Employees at the bank continually demonstrate their goal to "take your banking personally."

photo by tim barnwell

(Carolina First Bank continued from page 167)

state's western region, the bank opened two new Buncombe County offices in 2007 and broke ground on a six-story office building in the heart of downtown Asheville.

Yet, for Davis, a good bank has nothing to do with a building, a sign, or a name; it's about people. "Banking is not a commodity business. It's really not about money or finance; it's about humanity," he said. Billed as "a bank big enough to support you no matter how large you grow, but small

enough to respond without the red tape," Carolina First's people-oriented service and business model are attractive differentiators in the banking industry. The people at Carolina First don't believe in lip service; they believe that customer service is not a noun, but a verb. They demonstrate this claim with responsive attention to customer needs. "Decision makers want to deal with decision makers," said Davis. "At Carolina First, there are no long-distance phone calls or committees. You are dealing with a person who makes a decision over a desk and seals it with a handshake."

Whether personal, commercial, small-business, wealth management, or investor relations, the full-service Carolina First model is that of a super-community bank, meaning that one size fits all. The bank can be very responsive, making decisions locally, which is a strength claimed by most community banks. However, in addition, Carolina First has the capacity that many community banks don't have in terms of the ability to stimulate commerce in the community. "We can finance the mega shopping centers or equipment for the local barber shop," Davis explained.

That same capacity allows the bank to ingrain itself as a vital part of the community. Carolina First is a leader in the support of charitable causes and community development. For example, the bank recently made a major contribution to the University of North Carolina–Asheville (UNCA) for the building of the chancellor's residence, an important part of the UNCA facility. Davis extends community involvement to include his own time, because as a representative of his organization, action is paramount.

Davis recently joined the board of directors of the UNCA Foundation Board. He is the vice chairman of the economic development force in Asheville—AdvantageWest, an association with the mission of stimulating economic development in Western North Carolina. He also serves on the board of directors for the city's Health Adventure, the board of Hendersonville's Pardee Hospital, and on the North Carolina Banking Commission.

Recognizing the value of partnerships, putting customers first, and emphasizing innovation has resulted in many long-term alliances for Carolina First. "I don't want to be driven crazy with more details and forms at my bank. I just want simple answers. I want the bank to handle my needs. That's what I have with Carolina First," said Martha Lewis, president of Atlantic Physical Therapy. "They've kept every promise they've made to us. That's important to me . . . and to my congregation," stated Blakely N. Scott, pastor of the First Nazareth Baptist Church. Such statements are only a small sample of the positive testimonials regarding this bank. "There are bankers who work for banks and bankers who work for people," concluded Davis. Carolina First, of course, is proud to be the latter. ❖

photo by tim barnwell

▲ Due to the fast-paced growth in Buncombe County, Carolina First opened two new branches in 2007. This branch, under construction in Skyland, will be the third. The expansions reflect the company's success in personal, commercial, and small business banking and a respected reputation for wealth management and positive investor relations.

photo by rod reilly

photo by rod reilly

photo by scott indermaur

photo by rod reilly

photo by rod reilly

Nature's glory revealed

Asheville has been called the jewel of the Blue Ridge Mountains, and with good reason. Just look around. The city is nestled in a beautiful valley surrounded by breathtaking mountain views. Residents are always ready to take visitors on a guided tour, share their knowledge of local plants, recommend a favorite trail, suggest the best vantage point, or tell someone about a unique place to go and have fun. Locals claim that farms are more productive, cattle are fatter and give more milk, fish are just waiting to be caught, and that soaring over the landscape in a hot-air balloon is the only way to really see the area. There must be something to all those claims, because as far back as 1795, Asheville has been regarded as a place to rejuvenate both body and soul. With the introduction of the railroad in 1880, the word was out, and tourists and health seekers have been flocking to the area ever since.

ASHEVILLE CABINS OF WILLOW WINDS: it's all about location

photo by rod reilly

▲ A trip to Asheville Cabins of Willow Winds is a great opportunity not only to get back to nature, but also to enrich relationships with loved ones. For Colette Sipperly and her sons Jack, age four (middle), and Landon, age two-and-a-half (right), who hail from Upper Montclair, New Jersey, quality time fishing at the stocked trout pond has provided memories for a lifetime.

Is it really possible to get away from it all while being in the center of everything? It certainly is. And the proof is in the pudding, as they say, at Asheville Cabins of Willow Winds, an exquisite thirty-nine-acre secluded vacation rental retreat conveniently located within the city limits of Asheville and five minutes from the entrance to Biltmore Estate.

Featuring a charming collection of twenty-five rustic log and cedar resort cabins, Willow Winds has the only group of vacation rentals in North America located within a woodland garden. Bordered by the Blue Ridge Parkway and the Mountains-to-the-Sea Trail, Willow Winds provides guests with the peace and tranquility that nature affords while also offering easy access to the hustle and bustle of a truly exciting city. It's a distinctive dichotomy that has made the retreat stand out from all other lodging options in the region since it opened in 1997.

"Willow Winds is a unique property that has high standards of guest satisfaction. It strikes a unique balance of a serene woodland setting that is located just a few minutes from the dining and entertainment attractions of Asheville," explains Mike McLeod, who founded the resort with his wife Sandy after

(continued on page 174)

photo by scott indermaur

▲ For many visitors, hiking is a favorite activity at Willow Winds, thanks to the unspoiled trails that extend through the picturesque Woodland Gardens. Guests can also hike the Blue Ridge Parkway and the Mountains to the Sea Trail, which is easily accessible from the property.

◄ The views from the cabins on the property are unparalleled all year round. For instance, in the spring, the blooming rhododendron add a splash of color and beauty to the scenery that surrounds the popular Mom's Manor and Dad's Digs cabins.

photo by rod reilly

Willow Winds has the only group of vacation rentals in North America located within a woodland garden.

▲ A two-bedroom cabin at Willow Winds offers all of the comforts of home amongst the magnificence of the surrounding woods. Both well-appointed and cozy, a vacation rental property like this one offers guests of all ages the chance to put their feet up and savor some downtime, away from the hustle and bustle of everyday life.

photo by scott indermaur

(Willow Winds continued from page 173)

stumbling upon a twenty-acre tract of land that was not on the market but had been zoned for high-density housing development. When the couple discovered that the owner of the property did not want to sell it to a developer, they made an offer that included a promise to preserve the natural state of the land. Upon closing the deal, the McLeods started renovating the four houses that were situated there, converting them into vacation rental properties. Over the next several years, they purchased two adjoining tracts of land and built new cabins, bringing their total acreage to thirty-nine and their number of vacation rentals to twenty-five.

"Our cabins are equipped with all the comforts of home, including cable TV, high-speed Internet access, and a fully equipped kitchen," says Sandy. Tastefully decorated and furnished, the one-, two-, and three-bedroom cabins also boast everything from floor-to-ceiling fireplaces, large decks, and washer and dryer units, to hot tubs, porch rockers, electric barbeque grills, and access to Willow Winds' private mountain stream, complete with a waterfall and stocked trout pond. Additionally, the property offers many more amenities, such as the stunning woodland gardens, seven lighted fountains, a game porch, a putting green, two playgrounds, and nature trails. A walk along those trails is the perfect activity for visitors who love the great outdoors, especially since it offers an opportunity to encounter some of Mother Nature's most fascinating creatures. In fact, bird watching is a popular pastime for guests, with ducks, geese, cardinals, and a nesting pair of red-tailed hawks making appearances each year. It's just one of the features that regular visitor Jan Seitz looks forward to when she travels annually to Willow Winds with her husband, Tom.

"We found Willow Winds when we were hunting for a vacation spot in the mountains of North Carolina, and we really lucked out," Seitz explains. "The location is perfect. The cabins are very comfortable. Every year there's more landscaping added to the already beautiful grounds. And we always receive information regarding restaurants, sightseeing possibilities, and local events. It's just wonderful—I could go on and on."

That's what the McLeods like to hear. As Mike says, Willow Winds' philosophy is "to meet and exceed our guests' expectations." That viewpoint is shared by the resort's friendly and courteous full-time staff, which strives to make every visitor's stay as comfortable as possible. The team's efforts undoubtedly have made an impression on the guests who call Willow Winds home during their vacations in Asheville. "We needed a home away from home as we began construction on our house in Asheville. We discovered Willow Winds, and over the two years it took to complete our home, we made very dear friends of the staff," recall Bud and Brenna Kendrick. "And the excellent location close to the village, coupled with the natural forest atmosphere, which is so quiet and private, makes Willow Winds a rare find indeed."

Many guests not only come back year after year, but also book cabins in advance—some for the next ten years after staying at the property. By then, visitors will have even more to enjoy, as Mike, Sandy, and their son Chris continue to enhance Willow Winds with new amenities, upgraded landscaping, and more. As Sandy reveals, "We believe we have the most beautiful grounds of any vacation rentals, and the quality of our amenities, furnishings, and comforts are second to none. But we always try to make each year's experience even better than the last." ❖

photo by scott indermaur

▲ Little ones are not forgotten in the grand scheme of things at Willow Winds. In fact, there are a plethora of activities for younger guests to enjoy, with a water balloon station, horseshoes, and a game porch ready and waiting for the fun to begin. Youngsters, like the ones pictured here, can even get instructions on playing Bocce Ball, one of the property's many exciting pastimes.

▲ While enjoying the serenity of Willow Winds, it's hard not to be enchanted by the property's beautiful trout pond, where fishing enthusiasts can cast out a line for enjoyment or to catch dinner. And for those who prefer to sit back and relax, listening to the peaceful sounds of the flowing fountain or enjoying a good book by the water is a perfect way to spend the day.

photo by scott indermaur

photo by tim barnwell

photo by rod reilly

photo by rod reilly

(left page)

Not only are the rolling hills surrounding Asheville great for raising crops and livestock —and many families still make a living this way—they also provide a wonderful rural lifestyle for those who do other things. Or for those who choose, on occasion, to play hooky from work entirely and spend the day along a favorite fishing stream.

(right page)

People have always been fascinated with the idea of floating above the landscape, and what better way to do that than in a hot-air balloon? Approximately seventy-five hundred hot-air balloons operate in the United States, most used for recreation. Suspended in a wicker gondola, the passengers in this balloon get a chance to really enjoy Biltmore Lake and the lush forest that surrounds it. For those who like to keep their feet on the ground, the sixty-two-acre lake is surrounded by miles of shaded trails and walkways.

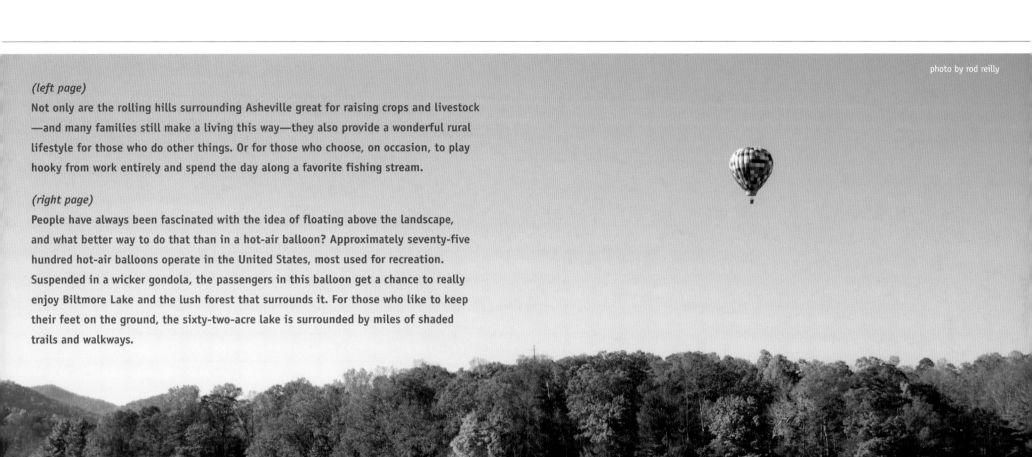

ALWAYS BEAUTIFUL: jewels that dance, an asheville treasure

photo by mario morgado

▲ The sleek, warm interior of Jewels That Dance welcomes
all shoppers.

A visit to Jewels That Dance, Asheville's oldest downtown jewelry gallery and custom design studio, is both a relaxing and a baffling experience. Relaxing in that the atmosphere is professional, but warm and inviting. Baffling in that the store is filled with so much beauty—platinum, gold, titanium, sterling, diamonds, fine gemstones, distinctive pearls, rings, bracelets, pendants, necklaces, engagement rings, and wedding bands—it is hard to know where to look.

A guided tour led by head designer, goldsmith, and co-owner Paula Dawkins or business partner Carol Schniedewind might be helpful. Suppose you inherited a piece of jewelry with several nice stones, but the setting is not to your liking.

"If you're a previous customer, we probably already know your taste and style," said Schniedewind. "We pride ourselves on that kind of personal service. If this is your first visit, we'd walk around the store looking at pieces to get an idea of what you like. Then I'd introduce you to Paula or one of our other designers. We do all our repairs and custom work in-house."

That harkens back to 1983 and the small downtown studio where Dawkins designed jewelry for the wholesale market. Now she and Schniedewind represent more than fifty designers in the gallery on Haywood Street. Time has brought other changes. Whereas designing a piece of custom jewelry used to begin with sketches, today it starts with digital goldsmithing. "Computer renderings allow us to work with customers anywhere," said Dawkins.

Although technology is opening new markets, the partners of Jewels That Dance plan to stay put, because they were among the first to invest their time, money, and talent in the downtown renaissance. "It's our knowledge and our expertise we plan to expand," said Dawkins.

To that end, she and store manager Marlene Clevenger recently traveled to South Africa to learn more about diamond mining. "My goal was to be able to assure our customers that our South African diamonds are conflict-free and that production is environmentally responsible. In addition to that, when someone purchases a diamond from us, we make a donation in their name to the Global Giving Foundation, which implements health and education programs in South Africa."

Closer to home, Jewels That Dance frequently gives back to the Asheville community by donating to nonprofit organizations. The staff also recently participated in an all-woman crew to build a house for Habitat for Humanity.

Another stop of our short tour of Jewels That Dance is the repair center. "We don't just sell jewelry. We build a relationship with our customers, and that involves not only designing, but caring for and repairing their jewelry," said Schniedewind. "Our designers can do marvelous things to repair and restore antique jewelry."

A quick tour of Jewels That Dance can only touch the surface, but visitors are invited to drop in anytime. There's always something new and beautiful to see. ❖

▲ Designer goldsmith Paula Dawkins brings life to each of her new designs.

photo by mario morgado

"If you're a previous customer, we probably already know your taste and style," said Schniedewind. "We pride ourselves on that kind of personal service."

During the 1929 Crash, Asheville suffered enormous financial hardship. For the next forty years, the tax base was small and city growth was slow, so tax monies went to more pressing needs than the destruction of old buildings. This turned out to be a blessing in disguise. In 1929, Asheville was a boom town, home for the Vanderbilts, a resort for Henry Ford, Thomas Edison, and others. Many of the original buildings are still in use in the downtown area, and include marvelous examples of Neoclassical, Romanesque Revival, Gothic, and Beaux Arts styles. Asheville also reputedly has more art-deco design work than any American city outside Miami Beach, Florida. Today visitors have only to look around to glimpse those bygone days.

all photos by mario morgado

With its fine attention to detail and sculpted features, the architecture

of downtown reveals the history of Asheville—a city both delightful and unique.

JOHNSON, PRICE & SPRINKLE PA, CERTIFIED PUBLIC ACCOUNTANTS:
taking initiative to improve the clients' positions

▲ The team members on the jobsite at one of JPS's Volunteer Days with Asheville Area Habitat for Humanity exemplify the dedication to the community as well as to their clients. JPS is a hometown certified public accounting firm with access to national and international expertise.

1. Established in 1955, enjoys a loyal client base and firm members dedicated to improving clients' positions.

2. Delivers the resources of a national firm but with regional firm service and state-of-the-art capabilities.

3. Progressive, responsive, and proactive. Principals and managers meet regularly with clients, many of whom become longtime friends of the firm, to discuss opportunities and planning considerations.

4. Enjoys valuable relationships with other business professionals and community involvement in its multiple marketplaces.

▲ A few of the JPS principals (left to right), Rollin Groseclose, Mickey Dale, Ben Hamrick, Leslie Johnson, Kathryn Atkinson, Scott Hughes, and Clement Hahn take a brief pause from a meeting held in the Asheville office. The CPA firm provides exemplary planning and advisory services to businesses—from small retailers to nonprofits to large corporations—across Western North Carolina.

These qualities capture the culture of certified public accounting firm Johnson, Price & Sprinkle PA (JPS). This regional accounting firm serves a roster of clients in the manufacturing, construction, real estate development, health-care, professional services, transportation, governmental/nonprofit, and retail/wholesale sectors, among others. Its target market is select—small to mid-size private companies, professional practices, individuals, and qualified nonprofit and governmental organizations in Western North Carolina. JPS has three offices conveniently located in Asheville, Hendersonville, and Marion.

The JPS service package is strategically designed to respond to the needs of its clientele. From providing business consulting, assurance services, tax planning and management services, business valuation and litigation support, technology services, financial planning, cost segregation studies, and small business services, to performance improvement consulting, analyses, and reporting, this firm boasts the resources of an international firm and thus offers an array of expertise unparalleled in the region. Technology-wise, the firm's savvy and conduct in this arena facilitates a leading-edge exchange of information with, and for, its clientele.

How does JPS differentiate itself from a host of qualified competitors? By emphasizing an approach that encompasses proactive consulting and planning as opposed to reactive compliance. What does this mean for clients? It assures an ongoing interest in them to a better position than when they first engaged the firm.

Through its affiliation with CPAmerica International, JPS is one of seventy-plus closely integrated firms across the nation with access to the expertise of fifteen thousand professionals in eighty-five countries around the world. Through JPS, you have access to national and international experts in your industry or business sector—all because of your relationship with the JPS folks right in your hometown.

The firm houses JPS Wealth Management, LLC, to provide nationally recognized and ranked financial planning and implementation services. Working with individuals and formed in 1999, JPS Wealth Management, LLC, provides a broad range of investment tools, insurance products, long-term financial planning, and trust services. While the array of products and services is vast, the advice is targeted and focused. This organization was ranked by *Research Magazine* as one of the top financial advisory services in the country and one of only twelve selected from the state of North Carolina. ✦

The JPS service package is strategically designed to respond to the needs of its clientele.

a man with a mission

Dr. Olson Huff, pediatrician and medical director emeritus of Mission Children's Hospital, is a man driven by his passion as an advocate for impoverished children and by an ongoing vision. "We need a health insurance program that will cover totally and completely every child in the United States," said Huff. He and his wife Marylyn have made North Carolina their family home since 1980, when Huff responded to an ad seeking a pediatrician for the state's developmental evaluation center. "It was a wonderful opportunity to be in the mountains, coupled with the opportunity to do the kind of medicine that I wanted to do—developmental pediatrics, which is my love," he said.

Developmental pediatricians work with children and young adults suffering from a variety of problems such as autism, brain injury, and learning and behavioral disorders. Huff entered this specialty as it was becoming a recognized field in pediatric medicine and has since channeled his zeal for his profession into a lifetime of helping children, both as a physician and by serving as their spokesperson.

Huff founded the Child Development Center, later renamed in his honor, and was instrumental in obtaining full funding for Asheville's new Reuter Children's Outpatient Center. As a senior fellow of Action for Children North Carolina, and his committed role with the American Academy of Pediatrics and the Committee on Federal Government Affairs, Huff helped to influence the federal government's reauthorization of a national children's health-care program.

Huff's book *The Window of Childhood* was adapted into a film, *Simple Things*, which won finalist status in the International Family Film Festival (IFFF). His numerous contributions to the welfare of children and honors received include the Lewis Hine Award, Asheville's Lifetime Achievement Community Service Award, and the Order of the Longleaf Pine, the highest civilian honor in the state.

Appreciative but humble regarding such accolades, Huff remains focused on his work as a consultant to Mission Healthcare Foundation, as the chair for the Task Force on Childhood Obesity, and as an emissary for children's health-care issues and preventive medicine.

Despite such continued community service, Huff affirms that he is retired. His assistant, Suzy Mayer, clarifies: "Retired? He's not seeing patients every day, but as an advocate and fund-raiser, he's busier than ever. He is still working for the children."

Dr. Olson Huff
*Pediatrician and Medical Director Emeritus
of Mission Children's Hospital*

A life devoted to children's health and well-being

photo by tim barnwell

GROCE FUNERAL HOME: assuring absolute integrity

photo by tim barnwell

▲ At a time when many funeral homes are owned by mega-corporations, Groce Funeral Home remains a local, family business. Representing the generations are *(standing from left)* Dale Groce and his wife Terrie, and Rhoda and her husband Bill Groce. Kristina Groce, the daughter of Dale and Terrie, is seated with Scott *(left)* and Trey Groce, sons of Bill and Rhoda.

At a time when many funeral homes are owned by mega-corporations, Groce Funeral Home remains a local, family business. "People come to us and are surprised to find that we act more like a neighbor than a business," said Bill Groce Jr. "We feel strongly that this allows us to serve Asheville families better and give them more personal attention."

Groce Funeral Home was founded in 1929 by the sons of Rev. T. A. Groce, one of the last circuit-riding Methodist ministers traveling in the mountains of Western North Carolina. "He started out in a horse and buggy and then moved up to a Model T Ford, which he said got around like an old horse," Dale Groce remembers. Bill and his brother Dale are the third generation of Groces in the business, and they are followed by Scott and W. H. ("Trey"), the fourth generation.

Due to their reputation for integrity and the efforts of a dedicated staff, Groce Funeral Home has become Buncombe County's largest funeral service provider. The property on Patton Avenue has gone through many changes over the years. The original building was built as a private home in the late 1920s. The chapel, the largest in Western North Carolina, was built in 1960, two large visitation rooms were added in 1985, and an off-premise cremation facility was added in 1996. In 1999, Groce dedicated their second location at Lake Julian in South Buncombe County.

Groce can arrange for national and international transfers, cremations, and prearrangements as well as traditional funerals which can be held either in the chapel, at the cemetery, or at the family's home church. "Over the years, we've conducted services for all religious denominations, military branches, and fraternal organizations."

While the Groces respect their heritage, they are also progressive and innovative. Their Web site provides obituary information and guest registers for families served in Western North Carolina and direct email messages to these families.

Groce Funeral Home was honored by the *Citizen-Times* readers as their choice for the Best Funeral Home in Western North Carolina for four consecutive years. Individuals, too, are lavish in their praise for the exceptional level of service extended by Groce.

(continued on page 188)

photo by tim barnwell

photo by tim barnwell

▲ Groce Funeral Home was founded in 1929 by the sons of Rev. T. A. Groce, one of the last circuit-riding Methodist ministers traveling in the mountains of Western North Carolina. Bill Groce *(seated)* and his brother Dale are the third generation of Groces in the business, and they are followed by Bill's sons, the fourth generation.

◀ W. H. (Trey) Groce *(left)* and his brother Scott are the fourth generation in what is truly a family-owned business. While the Groces respect their heritage, they are also progressive and innovative in providing the very best service to the families in Western North Carolina.

"People come to us and are surprised to find that we act more like a neighbor than a business."

Due to its reputation for integrity and the efforts of a dedicated staff, Groce Funeral Home has become Buncombe County's largest funeral service provider. Bob Hembree, senior staff director, is available to help families make decisions, whether the arrangements involve national and international transfers or a traditional funeral held in the chapel, at the cemetery, or at the family's home church.

photo by tim barnwell

(Groce Funeral Home continued from page 187)

One writes, "We were impressed with the warmth, attention to detail, and professionalism shown by the people who helped make the final arrangements. You and your staff thought about our needs and even anticipated things that we had not thought of."

Another family says, "We want to express our sincere appreciation for the way you helped us through the most difficult time in our history."

In addition to serving the needs of the community in times of bereavement, Groce Funeral Home actively supports the Asheville community in many other ways. The firm donates to dozens of charitable activities, including CarePartners Hospice and Four Seasons Hospice. The Groces and their staff members have held offices and memberships in the Chamber of Commerce, Better Business Bureau, North Carolina Board of Mortuary Science, and the North Carolina and National Funeral Directors Association.

Just as they have done in the past, by continuing to be both family-oriented and family-owned, the Groces anticipate that they will continue to provide funeral services for the citizens of the Asheville area through the twenty-first century. ❖

The original Central United Methodist Church was built in 1837. It was a small, white, one-story frame structure, and the basement was used for a female academy. Not until 1902 did construction begin on the current structure. Since that time it has been rebuilt, enlarged, renovated, and remodeled many times.

GOULD KILLIAN CPA GROUP, P.A., AND ALTAMONT CAPITAL MANAGEMENT, LLC:
partners in protecting and growing your assets responsibly

(Left to right) Harold Cole, Kathy Davis, Harvey Jenkins, Chuck Killian, and Ed Towson, officers of Gould Killian CPA Group, P.A.

photo by mario morgado

How many CPA firms do you know of that can trace their roots back to a conversation in a dugout during a Little League game? In 1998, while watching their sons play baseball, partners in two longtime Asheville CPA firms, dating back to the late 1960s, hit upon the idea to merge the two companies.

That idea reveals a lot about how Gould Killian does business. Distinguished by a diversity of resources and expertise, the firm takes a teamwork approach to its services, starting with a thorough understanding of a client's business and its needs. When necessary, Gould Killian also works as a member of a much larger team that includes a banker, attorney, insurance agent, and other professionals. The result is comprehensive accounting, bookkeeping, consulting, tax, and auditing services.

"Our services are defined by attention to detail, interest in the client, and a high level of technical expertise," says president Ed Towson. "We establish with our clients close working relationships that are both broad and deep. Many of our relationships stretch back decades."

photo by mario morgado

David Pheil, president of Altamont Capital Management.

ALTAMONT CAPITAL MANAGEMENT, LLC: A PARTNER IN GROWING YOUR ASSETS

Altamont is a Registered Investment Advisor Firm that specializes in developing long-term investment strategies for individual and institutional clients. Established by the Gould Killian partners and Altamont's managing partner and president, C. David Pheil, Altamont assists clients with growing their assets responsibly.

"Our clients are not speculative high-risk investors, but are already established financially," says Pheil. "We help them grow their assets over time while minimizing the numerous risks that abound in today's investment environment."

The ability to help clients protect and grow their assets makes Gould Killian CPA Group, P.A., and Altamont Capital Management, LLC, powerful partners for success. ❖

"Our services are defined by attention to detail, interest in the client, and a high level of technical expertise."

(right)

"We design buildings that are meaningful in time and place for the location and context, for the materials and the technology that go into each building, and that satisfy the goals of our clients as well," said Gene Edwards, Padgett & Freeman Architects partner. Edwards (left), Scott Donald, and Mike Freeman, also partners, stand before one of their flagship structures, the Asheville Chamber of Commerce and Visitors Center.

(below)

Located in the BB&T Building in downtown Asheville, Roberts & Stevens's team of twenty-six lawyers serve the citizens, businesses, and industries of the entire Western North Carolina region. In addition to providing a full spectrum of legal services, the firm represents a number of local school boards and provides specialty services to many others in the area.

photo by scott indermaur

photo by tim barnwell

MISSION HEALTH & HOSPITALS: lifesaving heart care

photo by mario morgado

▲ Cardiologist Brian H. Asbill, MD *(left)*, one of nearly thirty cardiologists in Asheville, chats with John Maize as he exercises at Mission's Heart Path cardiac rehabilitation program. Maize was recovering after successful quadruple coronary artery bypass surgery. More than one thousand cardiothoracic surgeries are performed at Mission Hospitals each year.

In 2005, a retired orthopedic surgeon flew to Asheville from Washington state to have a breakthrough heart procedure performed at Mission Health & Hospitals. He returned home days later, no longer plagued by atrial fibrillation.

Dr. Fred Moore may have traveled more miles than most to get to Mission, but thousands are given back their vigor for life—or life itself—thanks to Mission's award-winning heart program.

For six out of seven years, Mission has been named one of the nation's Top 100 Heart Hospitals by Solucient, the nation's leading source of health-care data. Other top national ratings came from *U.S. News & World Report*, HealthGrades, and Premier. Some of that recognition is the result of Mission's

investment in superb equipment and facilities, such as its heart tower and four cardiac catherization labs available around the clock. But beyond the rankings there is a thirty-five-year partnership between physicians of Asheville Cardiology Associates, Asheville Cardiovascular and Thoracic Surgeons, and Mission. Working closely with these physicians are teams of specialized nurses and technicians focused on providing state-of-the-art cardiovascular care with clinical outcomes comparable to any program—private or academic—in the United States.

For example, consider Mission's track record with defective heart valves. At the majority of large hospitals, about 80 percent of people treated for diseased heart valves receive artificial valves or tissue grafts that may fail and will require

(continued on page 194)

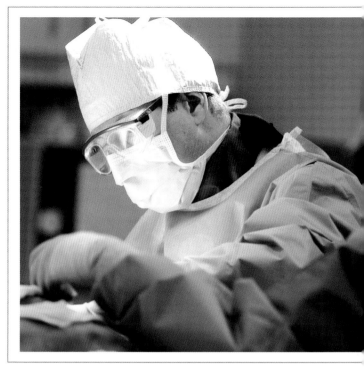

photo by mario morgado

▲ Pacemakers, automatic implantable cardiac defibrillators, and biventricular pacemakers for the treatment of heart failure are all placed at Mission Hospitals. Cardiac electrophysiologist Joseph J. Souza, MD, performs a pacemaker generator implantation.

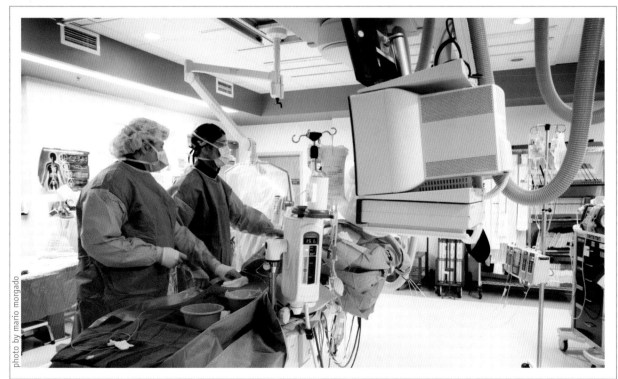

photo by mario morgado

◀ Mission offers round-the-clock emergency percutaneous coronary intervention with stent implantation, the treatment of choice for heart attack. Interventional cardiologist William T. Maddox, MD *(right)*, performs a catherization with assistance from cardiovascular technician Angela Solesbee. More than thirty-three hundred catheterizations and fourteen hundred coronary interventions are performed at Mission each year.

For six out of seven years, Mission has been named one of the nation's Top 100 Heart Hospitals by Solucient.

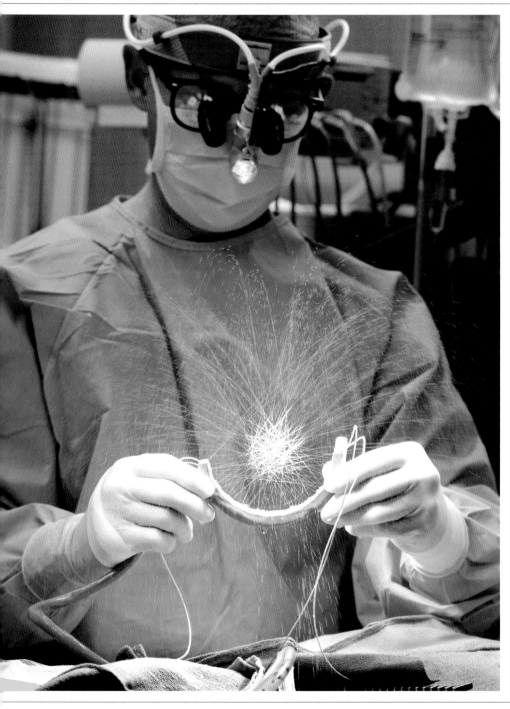

photo by blake madden

(Mission Health & Hospitals continued from page 193)

blood thinners for life. At Mission, the heart surgeons of Asheville Cardiovascular and Thoracic Surgeons are able to successfully repair 80 percent of the diseased heart valves they treat, a percentage far above the national average. "The benefits of repairing rather than replacing heart valves are significant," says heart surgeon Stephen Ely, co-chair of Mission's Heart Services. "Patients heal faster, have fewer long-term complications, and are often freed from a lifetime of anticoagulant therapy."

During a heart attack, quick response can mean the difference between full recovery and a lifetime of cardiac disability. The physicians of Asheville Cardiology Associates have significantly reduced the minutes it takes to get a patient to lifesaving stent placement in the cardiac catherization lab, regardless of day or time. In fact, Mission is a leader in North Carolina's RACE (Reperfusion in Carolina Emergency Departments) program, an effort to reduce the time-to-treatment in Asheville and all hospitals in Western North Carolina. Success in this area is in large part facilitated by Mission's Air Medical Ambulance and Regional Transport System.

"Asheville has an incredible level of medical care for a city its size," says cardiologist William Hathaway, co-chair of Mission's Heart Services and a partner in Asheville Cardiology Associates. "We offer a level of diagnostic sophistication and treatment capability you'd expect only in a teaching hospital. Complete diagnostic and therapeutic heart care, including coronary intervention, electrophysiology, and cardiac imaging, are available. This is augmented by top-rated, innovative surgical care. It's a standard set by the physicians who moved here a generation ago from major university settings to establish the Mission heart program. There is simply no need to seek cardiac care outside Asheville."

For complete information about Mission Health & Hospitals, Asheville Cardiology Associates, and Asheville Cardiovascular and Thoracic Surgeons, visit www.missionhospitals.org, www.avlcard.com, and www.avlcvsurgeons.com. ❖

Surgical and catheter-based ablation for the treatment of atrial fibrillation are available at Mission Hospitals. Cardiothoracic surgeon Mark Groh, MD, uses high-intensity focused ultrasound to perform ablation during heart surgery.

photo by rod reilly

The sun sets behind the Blue Ridge Mountains, bringing an end to another fulfilling day in Asheville. One of the region's most livable cities, Asheville is a place of rich culture and history, great natural beauty, and economic diversity.

The music scene illuminates the city's soul, offering something for everyone.

(far left)

For three decades, David Holt, a four-time Grammy winner, has performed and recorded with legends such as Doc Watson, Grandpa Jones, Earl Scruggs, and Chet Atkins. He and his band, the Lightning Bolts—shown jamming here at Asheville's Grove Park Inn—entertain audiences across America with mountain music and traditional tales that keep Southern lore alive.

(left)

Whether you are interested in a rock concert, a sporting event, a family show, the performing arts, an educational program, or even a convention coming to town, the destination is the same: the Asheville Civic Center. This facility is the heart of downtown Asheville's arts and entertainment scene. In addition to the variety of visiting shows, the Civic Center is home to three resident companies. For seventy-five years, Asheville Bravo Concerts has brought the best in musical, dance, and opera programs to Asheville. The Asheville Symphony also makes its home at the Civic Center, as does the Broadway in Asheville series.

gotta dance

Dance has always been a part of life in the Appalachians, and in Asheville there are plenty of opportunities for people of every generation to move to the beat. Local troupes offer instruction, performances, and outreach in dance styles ranging from experimental to jazz to ballet. Whether practicing in class, performing on stage, or taking their craft to the streets, Asheville's dancers share their love of the art with the community. One such group, the Asheville Contemporary Dance Theatre, a member of which stretches at the barre (right), encourages expression through dance with its family-friendly productions, presentations in schools, teaching residencies, and international exchange program. Founded in 1979, ACDT is the area's original modern dance company. For more than thirty years, the Asheville Ballet has also danced its way into Asheville's hearts through its annual production of The Nutcracker (pages 200 and 201). Held in the Diana Wortham Theatre, this classic is a highlight of the performances delivered annually by the Asheville Ballet Guild. The core of the guild consists of the professionals of the Ann Dunn & Dancers troupe. Beyond a regular season, the guild's activities include a dance camp, community involvement, special productions for area events, and classes at its Academy of Ballet and Contemporary Dance (page 199). Here, instructors like Wayne Burritt instill the love of dance into their eager students—even if he occasionally appears slightly exasperated.

photo by alan s. weiner

photo by thomas s. england

Dance till the stars
come down from the rafters.
Dance, Dance, Dance
till you drop.

~ W. H. Auden

WOLF MOUNTAIN REALTY — real estate services on a higher level

photo by tim barnwell

▲ You don't have to be a homeowner to enjoy views like this. Wolf Mountain Realty specializes in finding just that perfect vacation rental for those who want to make the most of Asheville's natural beauty and active lifestyle. Today, drinks on the deck with friends. Tomorrow, maybe some hiking, golf, or horseback riding.

Dinah Carver has spent most of her working life in the real estate industry. Today, she runs one of Western North Carolina's most successful realty and property management companies, Wolf Mountain Realty. What keeps her so enthused?

"It's the people," she says. "Their excitement when we find them their home, and hearing months, even years later that they're still excited to be there."

Assisted by her daughter Connie Carver, herself a veteran of the industry, and a team of knowledgeable brokers and managers, Dinah and Connie have grown Wolf Mountain Realty into one of the most successful realty, property management, and resort rental companies in the region.

Located outside Mars Hill, Wolf Mountain Realty specializes in helping clients find that perfect property, whether it's a new home or a stylish condominium, a primary residence or a vacation rental. For homeowners seeking to rent their properties, Wolf Mountain provides a full spectrum of property management services, including security and grounds maintenance.

"The main thing we sell is service," Dinah says. "We don't just sell someone a property and then leave them to fend for themselves. We provide all kinds of direct assistance as well as referrals for additional needs."

While Wolf Mountain Realty serves clients throughout North Carolina and Tennessee, the company is also one of the primary real estate agencies for Wolf Laurel Resort. A secured residential community of five thousand acres located twenty-seven miles north of Asheville, Wolf Laurel Resort exemplifies the wooded privacy, high elevation, and active outdoor lifestyle that draw many to the region. The resort is home to Wolf Laurel Golf and Country Club, is located only minutes from the scenic Wolf Ridge Ski Resort, and is surrounded on three sides by National Forest and its dozens of hiking and horseback riding trails.

"People who move here like the idea that the summers are cool and that there are so many outdoor amenities," says Connie. "We're selling not only views and elevation, but also a relaxed lifestyle, one where people can let their hair down and escape from the hustle and bustle."

In addition to its property sales, Wolf Mountain Realty has the largest resort rental program in Wolf Laurel Resort, providing clients with vacation rental cabins, mountain chalets, and condominiums. The company also services some rentals outside the resort.

Born and raised in the region, Dinah works to help its communities remain livable and welcoming for residents and visitors alike. She and her company regularly contribute to a variety of local social and cultural initiatives, including the Southern Appalachian Repertory Theatre (SART) and Mars Hill College. Wolf Mountain has also collected pennies for My Sister's Place in Madison County as part of their One Million Pennies for domestic violence campaign.

Dinah doesn't take her success for granted. Instead, she continues to commit herself to the hard work and long hours needed to allow her clients to discover what she calls that special Western North Carolina feel—one that makes the region such a great place to visit and put down roots. ❖

▲ For this threesome, sinking a difficult putt is just icing on the cake during a day out at Wolf Laurel Golf and Country Club. There are virtually no parallel fairways at this eighteen-hole championship course, which allows for exceptionally private play amid a beautiful forest setting. After play, members and guests can enjoy refreshment at the five-thousand-square-foot clubhouse and lounge.

photo by rod reilly

"People who move here like the idea that the summers are cool and that there are so many outdoor amenities."

photo by rod reilly

(left page)
You can expect to find everything from the quaint to the quirky at Not Your Average Antiques, an Asheville shop featuring pottery and folk art, guitars and glass art, figurines and furniture, and much, much more.

(right page)
Built twenty years prior to the Civil War by successful businessman James McConnell Smith and later purchased by his business partner and son-in-law, William Wallace McDowell, Asheville's first mansion, the Smith-McDowell House, is now a beautifully restored period museum. As Asheville's oldest surviving structure and the oldest brick home in Buncombe County, the museum houses significant historical objects of Western North Carolina life from 1840 to 1890. Historic period interpreter Robert "Doc" Halliday is also on hand during tours to bring to life the colorful anecdotes surrounding one of Asheville's great architectural and historical treasures.

WCU: connecting education, engagement, and economic development

▲ Zak Kuhn (right), a student majoring in manufacturing engineering, and Professor Monty Graham work with WCU's $580,000 precision laser system—one of the high-tech tools the university uses to give students career-related experience and to assist business and industry.

"What we're seeing in this generation of students is a real hunger for meaning."

Western Carolina University students enter as individuals curious for knowledge and leave as graduates well prepared to contribute to the economic development of their communities. "A student with a Western education should live our state's motto, *Esse Quam Videri* — that is, 'to be, rather than to seem,'" explains chancellor John Bardo.

Western is one of a handful of universities implementing "synthetical education"—a centuries-old concept that encourages educators to help students relate what they learn in the classroom to the world around them. "The fundamental nature of the university is to engage with our region for the purpose of improving teaching, scholarship, and service through our focus on community economic development. What we're really trying to do is develop regional competence—the ability to respond to changing conditions," Bardo explains. Western combines a quality traditional education with practical experience in a variety of settings. Consequently, students develop the capacity to think critically and apply what they have learned to community issues.

"What we're seeing in this generation of students is a real hunger for meaning," the chancellor says. "This type of education provides the framework to help WCU students understand the value of what they are learning and the meaning of their education," he says. "It's one thing to have memorized Aristotle; it's another thing to know why it is important." With that combination, Western and its graduates are uniquely positioned to serve the needs of the region, the state, and the world. ❖

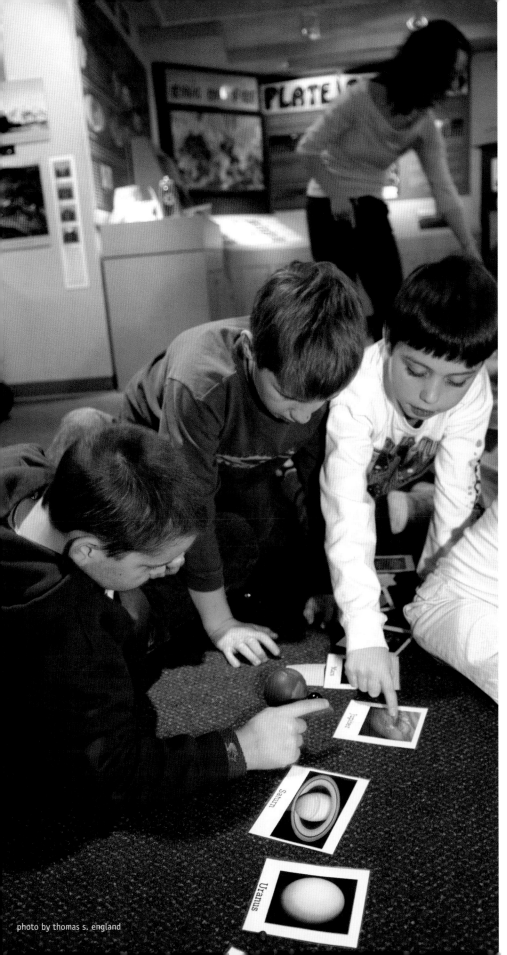

photo by thomas s. england

photo by thomas s. england

(above)

Upper School students combine art with global studies. At Carolina Day School, learning isn't just about preparing for college, but about setting the foundation for discovery throughout one's life. So running a race at a track meet becomes an opportunity to explore the nature of discipline. Preparing an oral report offers invaluable lessons in communication. Even an art project can bring students like these seniors a renewed understanding of the world around them.

(left)

Located inside the Pack Place Education, Arts & Science Center in downtown Asheville, the Colburn Earth Science Museum is a place where visitors can explore a fascinating collection of some forty-five hundred rocks and minerals from around the world. The center's collections also include fossils, crystals, and more than one thousand cut gemstones, ranging from a 220-carat blue topaz to a 2,000-plus-carat opal. Through the center's interactive exhibit on the weather and climate, or its unique education programs, kids can also learn about the planets, the atmosphere, and more.

GIVENS ESTATES — redefining retirement community living

▲ Water aerobics is just one of the many classes offered on a continuing basis at Givens Estates. From crafts and concerts to dancing and day trips, there are plenty of opportunities for residents to stay active. In addition to scheduled activities, residents can also find individual fulfillment using the on-campus library, greenhouse, game courts, trails, and more.

From its idyllic mountain setting, Givens Estates United Methodist Retirement Community offers seniors a place for life, celebrating active living. Founded in 1975, Givens is open to everyone regardless of faith or income level.

An abundance of living options are available to suit any preference or financial criteria. For seniors enjoying independence, Givens offers four distinct housing options, each balancing security and privacy with a sense of community. Whether it's a free-standing cottage, house, duplex, or villa, there are numerous floor plans and a variety of neighborhoods for full independent living.

Givens also offers various apartment styles with many conveniences located in the same building that range from multiroom residences with more than eighteen hundred square feet to smaller, more affordable studios with kitchenettes. Residents with limited resources may qualify for a more affordable subsidized apartment.

Regardless of residence, life at Givens Estates is free of worry over issues such as landscaping, maintenance, or housekeeping. This freedom allows residents more time to enjoy amenities like the library, computer center, greenhouse and gardening plots, trails for hiking and walking, woodworking shop, art and pottery studios, swimming pool and fitness center, chapel, and performing arts center.

Culinary excellence makes dining at Givens a source of delight. Options include indoor and outdoor casual dining with a mountain view, elegant fine dining, take-out selections, and available catering for in-home entertainment.

In fact, Givens's residents are a highly active group, taking part in regularly scheduled activities including exercise and art classes, shopping trips, cultural outings, and Bible study. Many take advantage of the varied offerings at the college for seniors, affiliated with the Center for Creative Retirement at UNC-Asheville. Volunteer opportunities with a host of organizations and community projects also provide a rewarding place to put the residents' considerable talents to good use.

As a community that places great emphasis on wellness and quality of life, Givens Estates provides the full continuum of services to meet changing and sometimes challenging health-care needs. In addition to an emergency call system readily available in all residences, the community offers campus nursing services, clinic, home care, and transportation to health-related appointments.

For those in need of additional support with daily activities, the Richard A. Wood Assisted Living Center offers care and encouragement in a lovely residential surrounding. Complete skilled nursing services are available at the Givens Health Center in the Sales Nursing wing. And, for those in need of special assistance with memory-related challenges, there is the Starnes Special Care wing.

Individuals who choose Givens Estates are planners who appreciate the gracious lifestyle, security, and value this community offers. ✣

Givens Estates' various housing options are designed for residents who enjoy independent, active lifestyles. While features and services vary depending on type of residence, each offers a private, secure place to call home within a lushly landscaped community.

Givens offers four distinct housing options, each balancing security and privacy with a sense of community.

photo by tim barnwell

(left page)
Considered one of the top eleven scenic drives in Asheville, a trip to Beaver Lake in the spring rewards visitors with a spectacular burst of color as the surrounding trees, like this dogwood, start their bloom. To catch spring wildlife of another sort, visitors on the first Saturday of every month should be sure to augment their trip with a guided bird walk at the Beaver Lake Audubon Bird Sanctuary.

(right page)
For some of the best Italian food in Black Mountain, head over to My Father's Pizza & Pasta, where the popularity of the pizza alone makes this one of the busiest restaurants in town. Black Mountain residents Pam and Worth Hester have also discovered other culinary offerings while enjoying the restaurant's outdoor seating.

THE RENAISSANCE EXPERIENCE — defined by local color and gracious service

photo by rod reilly

▲ Designed and built by a local architect and contractor, the light and bright sixty-foot lap pool and Jacuzzi bring the outdoors indoors. The onsite fitness center with its cardiovascular equipment and free weights also provides guests with additional opportunities to keep fit during their stay.

Whether traveling for business or for pleasure, guests who stay at the Asheville Renaissance Hotel experience a unique quality of service. Located in the heart of downtown Asheville, the Renaissance combines the down-home friendliness of a bed-and-breakfast with the savvy sophistication of an internationally recognized hotel brand.

The Renaissance is aptly named. In 1998, Windsor Capital Group purchased the hotel and began an ongoing, multimillion-dollar plan to make the hotel the upscale property it is today. This includes a sixty-foot indoor pool, Jacuzzi, state-of-the-art exercise facility, outdoor dining space, and a third ballroom culminating in approximately twenty thousand square feet of total meeting space. As a division of Marriott hotels, the Renaissance name, along with Marriott Ritz-Carlton, is synonymous with high-end hotel properties.

The resulting "Renaissance Experience" reflects better than ever the stellar service and amenities expected from the Marriott name, as well as the charming character of Asheville and its environs.

Not only do the 275 guest rooms provide the ultimate in comfort and privacy, they are also designed to provide a host of home-away-from-home amenities. The concept, known as the Room That Works®, includes in-room high-speed Internet access, satellite/cable television on thirty-two-inch flat-screen LCD televisions, two-line telephones with voice messaging, work desk, and coffee/tea maker. In keeping with Asheville's commitment to a better environment, the hotel also features a number of green products, from organic cotton bedding to biodegradable soaps and shampoos.

The Asheville Renaissance Hotel, very much a part of the downtown scene, is the only hotel in the area that offers such exceptional service within walking distance of the best the city has to offer. On-site fine dining is available for breakfast, lunch, and dinner at the Orchards restaurant, or guests may explore any number of nearby eateries. The staff is also exceptionally knowledgeable about local attractions, from art galleries to hiking trails to the famed Thomas Wolfe Memorial, located just next door.

A vital part of the city's economy, the hotel has embraced a community-focused philosophy since its inception, utilizing local contractors and labor for both renovations, filling the property with locally produced arts and crafts, and, whenever possible, purchasing from local suppliers. The work of local artisans hangs in all the guest rooms, and the hotel's identity piece was commissioned and designed by a local artist.

In an effort to achieve ongoing goals of strong, local community involvement, the hotel focuses on supporting the arts community in the downtown and local area.

Located in the heart of downtown, the Asheville Renaissance Hotel is as unique as the community it serves. It excels at offering business and pleasure travelers the finest in full-service accommodations and amenities that make for a better stay, while also building relationships with local businesses and attractions that make for a better quality of life. ❖

▲ With over twenty-one thousand square feet of total meeting space, including fifteen rooms and an eighty-one-hundred-square-foot Grand Ballroom seating over five hundred people, the Renaissance is able to meet any event and meeting need. Catering and certified wedding planning services are also available to help guests plan and coordinate their event from start to finish.

photo by rod reilly

Not only do the 275 guest rooms provide the ultimate in comfort and privacy, they are also designed to provide a host of home-away-from-home amenities.

In Asheville it's all about style. And when it comes to local style, the place to be is Lexington Avenue. Residents like Rob Russell and Tracey Anne Berry (shown here enjoying a coffee break at Izzy's Coffee Den) and Flipside Boardshop store owner, Krista Parham, agree with their neighbors who rate Lexington Avenue the best place to buy books, art, women's clothing, crafts, art supplies, antiques, and even health-conscious groceries. And that's just on a normal day. Then there's LAAFF. The annual Lexington Avenue Arts and Fun Festival is a one-day event that shows off everything local to its best advantage.

photo by scott indermaur

DEERFIELD — live the retirement of your dreams

▲ Nestled on 110 wooded acres adjoining the beautiful Blue Ridge Parkway, Deerfield Episcopal Retirement Community has been a constant and caring presence in Asheville since 1955.

Deerfield Episcopal Retirement Community embraces the belief that when one door in life closes, another opens to reveal even more wonderful opportunities. Through a variety of living options, stimulating activities, and high-quality, long-term medical services, residents are ensured an active, independent, and worry-free retirement.

Located on 110 acres just south of Asheville, Deerfield was established in 1955 by the Episcopal Diocese of Western North Carolina at the urging of Bishop George Henry as a retirement home for the elderly. Guided by Christian ideals since its founding, Deerfield has also become Asheville's only comprehensive LifeCare community, providing a continuum of care for its residents at every stage of life.

Independent living options include one- and two-bedroom apartments, cottages, villas, and cluster homes. For those requiring support in their daily activities, Deerfield's Health and Wellness Center features forty assisted-living suites in a homelike atmosphere, while the Skilled Nursing Center provides forty-eight private rooms with twenty-four-hour care. Once completed, the community's latest expansion project will add an additional eighty-two independent-living apartments, additional health-care residences, and expanded community spaces.

No matter their level of independence, all residents enjoy a host of amenities that ensure a worry-free lifestyle. Included in the monthly fee are utilities, one daily meal, weekly housekeeping, maintenance and grounds keeping, twenty-four-hour security and emergency assistance, transportation, and visits to Deerfield's clinic.

Deerfield also provides residents with a wide range of mental, physical, social, and spiritual enrichment. The health and wellness center includes not only a weight room, lap pool, croquet court, and a number of exercise classes, but also the community's physical, occupational, aquatic, and speech therapy programs.

Noted for the quality of its food and dining services, Deerfield provides casual dining at its café-like Bistro, with convenient hours, buffet-style service, and even takeout meals. Guests seeking a more intimate experience may reserve a table in the Fine Dining Room. Private dining rooms are also available for special occasions, and the terrace is the site of al fresco meals in the warm months.

Sociability is further encouraged by plenty of common space, an active volunteer program, and excursions to nearby Asheville attractions. An on-site computer lab, library, and continuing educational programs encourage residents to pursue their hobbies and interests or establish entirely new ones.

Deerfield is also one of the few retirement communities in the country with its own freestanding chapel and full-time chaplain. Located near the community's front entrance, the St. Giles chapel provides Wednesday afternoon and Sunday morning Episcopal worship services while also incorporating the traditions of other religious faiths.

In fact, Deerfield cherishes its diversity. Half of its residents come from outside the region and represent many different walks of life. The resulting environment—lively, stimulating, inclusive—is what most likely prompted one resident to call life at Deerfield like summer camp for adults.

Certainly, retirement means different things to different people. Deerfield capably accommodates those differences while never compromising its core mission: to ensure each resident a life of independence, dignity, and vitality.

photo by alan s. weiner

Fun and stimulating, Aquacize in the 4,755-square-foot Aquatic Center is just one of the many activities that enhance life for the residents of Deerfield. Also available are Pilates, Tai Chi, yoga, hiking, Nordic walking, multiple aerobic classes, and croquet.

No matter their level of independence, all residents enjoy a host of amenities that ensure a worry-free lifestyle.

all photos by mario morgado

local artisans merge the past and the present

Since the earliest of times, the mountains of North Carolina have been a prolific source of beautifully handcrafted pieces of art, from quilts, furniture, and pottery to clothing and jewelry. Today, Asheville's local artisans are keeping the traditions of yesteryear alive by continuing to craft coveted pieces of artwork using all kinds of media, including ceramics, blown glass, wrought iron, turned wood, fiber, and metal, among many other materials—all with their own present-day twist. And these items are showcased in the many galleries and shops found throughout the city. Along such main streets as Biltmore Avenue and Boston Way, visitors can peruse captivating displays of traditional and contemporary pieces at places like the Allanstand Craft Shop (this page and opposite), Blue Spiral 1 (page 220), New Morning Gallery, Bellagio, 16 Patton Fine Art, and the Ariel Craft Gallery (page 221), and walk away with a true treasure. Even outside of the downtown area, galleries abound, with locales like the Miya Gallery in nearby Weaverville presenting a wide array of engaging creations. The Asheville Art Museum is another wonderful place to take in the inspired handicrafts that have become synonymous with Asheville, North Carolina, and the Blue Ridge Mountains. For a city with a history so rich in the visual arts, it's no wonder that Asheville's gallery scene is one of its finest amenities.

photo by mario morgado

oday, Asheville's local artisans are keeping the traditions of yesteryear alive by continuing to craft coveted pieces of artwork with their own present-day twist.

UNITED WAY OF ASHEVILLE AND BUNCOMBE COUNTY:
strengthening our community since 1921

photo by scott indermaur

▲ United Way funds more than ninety programs designed to strengthen the community with a mission of Helping Children and Families Succeed, Improving Peoples' Health, and Promoting Independence and Stability. The YWCA Daycare program provides children a safe and nurturing place to learn. Visit www.unitedwayabc.org to learn more.

From its early beginnings as the Community Chest through the adoption of its community-focused funding councils, United Way has given people who want to help strengthen our community a chance to do so, whether through gifts of time, talent, or money.

This commitment is evidenced in the nonprofit programs that receive United Way funding and in the lives those programs change. Our focus is on effecting lasting change by:

- Helping children and families succeed
- Improving people's health
- Promoting independence and stability

United Way volunteers are active year-round, learning about community needs, bringing people together to identify and support solutions, or raising money to fund local non-profits. Together, they make a difference in our community, every day. United Way's community service programs, United Way's 2-1-1 of Western North Carolina (WNC) and Hands On Asheville-Buncombe, allow people to get and give help.

2-1-1 (cell phones dial 252-HELP) is a free, confidential information line that links people to health and human services. Available 24/7 in Buncombe, Henderson, Transylvania, and Madison counties, 2-1-1 makes it easy for callers to find the help they need. 2-1-1's database is searchable online at www.211wnc.org.

Hands On Asheville-Buncombe makes it easy to lend a hand and help others in our community by volunteering. Visit www.handsonasheville.org or call 2-1-1 and choose the volunteer opportunity that works for you. Volunteer on your own or with your family, business, or faith community.

By bringing the community together, United Way strengthens our community by helping people improve their lives and care for one another. ❖

Together, they make a difference in our community, every day.

Carrier Park, on the French Broad River, offers volleyball and basketball courts, trails and sports fields, roller hockey, and a multiuse track that hosts a popular cycling race series. Conversion of the track, a one-third-mile oval formerly used by automobile racers, is one of many developments in the park. Plans for the future include additional trails, improvements along the river, picnic areas, and more.

photo by scott indermaur

A-B TECH: offering innovative career opportunities

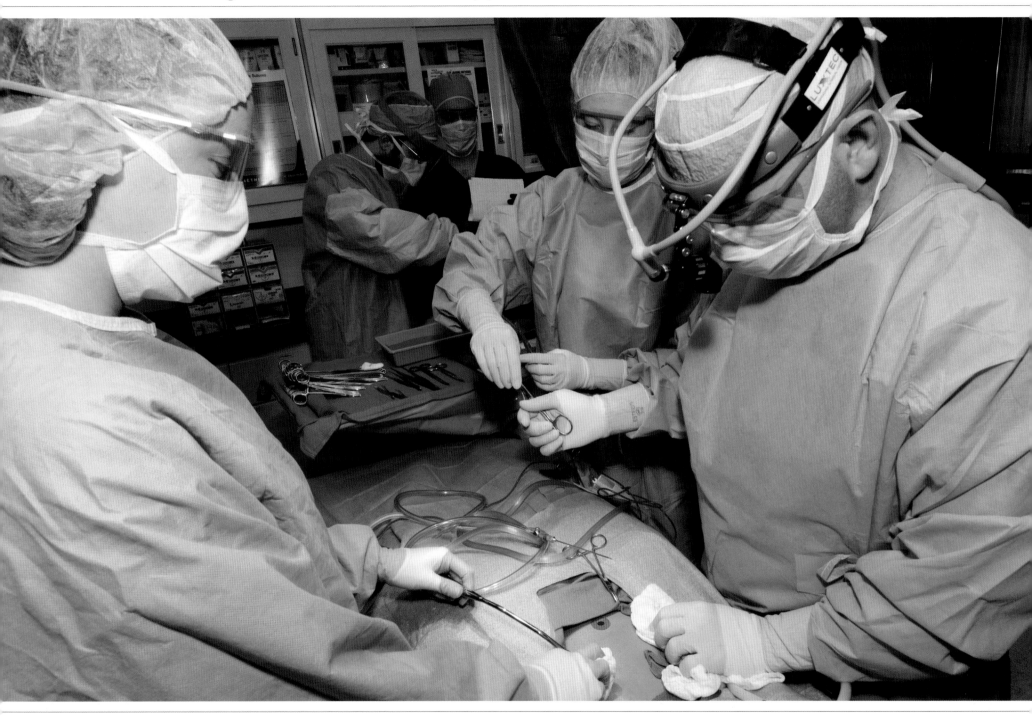

photo by thomas s. england

A-B Tech's surgical technology program prepares students to help meet the demands of the region's burgeoning health-care industry.

From its beginnings as an industrial education center in 1959, Asheville-Buncombe Technical Community College has grown into a comprehensive community college that enrolls more than twenty-six thousand students, giving it the largest headcount of any institution of higher education in Western North Carolina. Recognized for its dedication to student success, the college offers more than fifty innovative career programs, along with college transfer degrees and more than twelve hundred continuing education courses.

A-B Tech awards associate's degrees, diplomas, and certificates through four academic divisions: Allied Health and Public Service Education, Arts and Sciences, Business and Hospitality Education, and Engineering and Applied Technology. A fifth division, Continuing Education, offers opportunities for specific job training and retraining, basic skills education, and avocational courses for individual enrichment.

With more than nine thousand curriculum students and seventeen thousand in Continuing Education, A-B Tech is ranked among the fastest-growing community colleges in the country. The college has three campuses located in Buncombe and Madison counties, as well as a new two-classroom site at the Asheville Mall.

A-B Tech has received superior ratings on state performance measures mandated by the General Assembly to ensure that North Carolina's community colleges offer quality programs and services. The results show high satisfaction rates among students for the quality of the college's programs and services, and among employers for the performance of the students they hire. Business and industry also indicate their satisfaction with the services the college provides.

The Magnolia Hospitality Education Center, with four kitchens and a 120-seat demonstration hall, serves as a state-of-the-art training facility for students in A-B Tech's award-winning culinary program. Student teams have won state, regional, and national honors in the American Culinary Federation's Hot Food competitions.

The demand for Allied Health programs is expected to grow by 38 percent during the next decade. A-B Tech's partnership with Mission Hospitals allows the college to provide for growth of existing high-demand allied health programs and the addition of new programs to meet the region's rapidly growing need for highly trained allied health professionals.

Students in several Engineering and Applied Technology programs at A-B Tech work together to build modular housing for nonprofit organizations. Construction management technology students oversee construction of the units by carpentry, air conditioning and heating, electronics engineering technology, civil engineering, welding, and CAD technology students. Students build the homes, which are sold at cost to affordable housing agencies.

A-B Tech also has transfer agreements with many four-year institutions, allowing students to complete the first two years of college while paying affordable tuition and receiving a quality education.

Located at A-B Tech's Enka campus, the Center for Corporate and Economic Development houses a corporate technology training and conference center, a technology commercialization center, a biotechnology incubator, and a small business center and incubator. The campus was created in 2000 when textile maker BASF donated thirty-seven acres and three buildings containing 277,000 square feet to A-B Tech. Then-Governor Jim Hunt said the gift was the largest donation of property to a community college in the country. ❖

Students in the Baking and Pastry program at A-B Tech practice their artistry on heart-shaped wedding cakes. Baking and Pastry is one of three programs in the nationally renowned hospitality education department. Degrees also are offered in culinary technology and hotel and restaurant management.

photo by thomas s. england

Recognized for its dedication to student success, the college offers more than fifty innovative career programs.

photo by thomas s. england

photo by thomas s. england

photo by tim barnwell

photo by thomas s. england

photo by rod reilly

celebrate variety

Asheville festivals and competitive events represent a full variety of interests. For those who want to be immersed in memories of days gone by, there are heritage and holiday festivals that take revelers back to the nineteenth century and earlier. Take, for instance, the Biltmore Village Dickens Festival. Held the first weekend in December, this festival magically transports visitors back to a quaint nineteenth-century Victorian village where the likes of David Copperfield, Oliver Twist, and Ebenezer Scrooge are strolling down the streets. For people with a taste for competition, there are contests to award the best in everything from baking to wine-making to cross-country horse racing. One of these delightful contests is the National Gingerbread House Competition, which takes place every November at the Grove Park Inn Resort and Spa. And with so much natural beauty, there is no end to the outdoor competitions to be found for the pro, the amateur, or even the armchair athlete. These outdoor sporting events typically give competitors the chance to run the distance, bike through the mountains, paddle the area's waterways, or take part in any number of other athletic activities. Ask anyone in Asheville, and they will tell you part of the attraction of living here is that there is always something to do.

BLUE RIDGE LIMOUSINE — where every client is a VIP

photo by mario morgado

Asheville is becoming an increasingly popular destination wedding spot, and Blue Ridge Limousine excels at transporting wedding parties in comfort and style. This Lincoln Town Car stretch can hold up to ten passengers. It features red carpet service, crystalware, lighted coolers, fiber optics, custom walnut accent trims, mirrored privacy divider, flat-screen monitors, DVD player, premium sound system with CD player, and the coldest A/C in the South.

Since it was established in 2003, Blue Ridge Limousine has become one of Asheville's most successful ground transportation companies. But you won't find founder and CEO Gilbert Santiago resting on his laurels any time soon. Customer service, he believes, is an ongoing commitment. Whether transporting an Arab sheik who tips in Rolex watches or a high school junior attending her first prom, each client is provided nothing less than a first-class experience.

Born and raised in New York City, Santiago arrived in Asheville in 1994 via South Beach, where he honed his skills in service-oriented industries such as firefighting, ground transportation, and restaurant management. One day, a friend living in Asheville called to ask for Santiago's help in opening a restaurant. Within weeks, he'd found his new home.

"I had the same feeling about Asheville I had about South Beach," he says. "It was just a matter of time before people discovered what a great place it is. I knew there would eventually be a market in this town for what I wanted to do."

Having learned the ins and outs of first-class ground transportation service in Miami, Santiago wanted to bring to Asheville a superior car service company geared toward an upscale market but at competitive prices. With no advertising except word-of-mouth, he grew his business from one sedan to a fleet of seven, including a Mercedes van that runs on biodiesel, thus becoming the region's first eco-friendly limousine/ transportation company. Blue Ridge has since emerged as the preferred choice for visitors and businesspeople throughout Western North Carolina.

"The recipe for success is pretty simple," says Santiago. "First of all, clients want a company that shows up on time.

And that means fifteen minutes early. They also want a clean car and a courteous, knowledgeable driver."

Santiago doesn't necessarily hire drivers with previous limousine experience. "I would much rather hire someone with a service background and convert those skills into those of a chauffeur. We like to say that our clients experience the kind of service found at a fine dining establishment. Only instead of dinner, we serve them a first-class transportation experience."

Because Blue Ridge caters to a large number of corporate and upscale clientele, attention to detail is a must. The company keeps meticulous records of its regular clients' likes and dislikes and special dates such as birthdays and anniversaries. It does extensive research on new clients while keeping in mind that discretion and privacy are of the highest priority. Drivers also stay up-to-date on whatever is going on in both Asheville and throughout the region.

While still growing his own business, Santiago is also mindful to contribute to the community that's brought him so much success. He gives back in some way at least once a week, and is especially devoted to children's and school-related initiatives.

"Our goal is to serve our clients at every point in their lives—as newborns going home from the hospital, when they go to prom, when they graduate college, when they get married," Santiago says. "We're a company that looks to the future. Our relationships are for the long term." ❖

▲ Owner Gilbert Santiago's diverse fleet of vehicles accommodates a wide variety of client needs, with a biodiesel van perfect for large parties, elegant stretch limos for once-in-a-lifetime occasions, and luxury sedans that provide business clients the ultimate in comfort and reliability.

photo by mario morgado

Blue Ridge has since emerged as the preferred choice for visitors and businesspeople throughout Western North Carolina.

(left page)

Southern comfort is personified at the Tupelo Honey Café, one of Asheville's most charming and inviting local eateries. Seamlessly blending the allure of an old-fashioned tearoom with the excitement of an upscale restaurant, the downtown eatery was opened in December 2000 by native southerner Sharon Schott.

(right page)

In a city like Asheville, which nurtures and encourages artists of all kinds, it not surprising to see examples of that creativity everywhere. Sculpture runs the gamut from whimsical garden art to a boy on stilts striding through downtown, or even a lone cat creeping along a wall.

GRATEFUL STEPS: giving back for its blessings

photo by thomas s. england

▲ At Grateful Steps, bringing a book to publication is a team effort. *(Left to right)* Business manager Lindy Gibson, photographer Michael Oppenheim, owner/publisher Micki Cabaniss Eutsler, Asheville architect/historian Richard Hansley, and marketing director Tom Scheve discuss Oppenheim's photos for inclusion in a recent photo book, *Look Up Asheville*.

Micki Cabaniss Eutsler, author of a medical textbook with a major publisher, decided to develop several general-interest books upon retirement from the practice of obstetrics. In the process, she founded Grateful Steps, an Asheville-based book publishing company that helps individuals and businesses throughout Western North Carolina bring their stories to light.

"So many people have wonderful stories to tell," she explains, "but because they don't have a journalism background or know the publishing industry, they encounter obstacles. We guide them around those obstacles through what we ourselves have learned and are continuing to learn."

A team effort includes daughter Michele Scheve as art director, son-in-law Tom Scheve as marketing director, and Lindy Gibson as business manager. Skilled off-site copyediting is provided by stepson Dan Cabaniss. Grateful Steps assists authors with every step to turn their rough ideas into professional publications. Its services include market and audience analysis; copyediting, layout, and design; and marketing, distribution, and direct sales. In developing contracts with illustrators and other consultants and for printing and binding, Asheville talent and businesses are prioritized.

Works in process run the gamut from collections of poetry and photography to self-help gift books, novels, autobiographies, and a biblical reference book. Not a religious publishing company in the strict sense, Grateful Steps does operate from a Christian-based philosophy that informs every aspect of the business. "It's more a statement of our ethics, a way of doing business," says Eutsler.

That way is inherent in the company's mission: to give thanks by helping authors and illustrators realize their publishing dreams and, in the process, highlight the wonderful stories told by and about the people of Western North Carolina. ❖

◄ Grateful Steps proudly supplies one-on-one support for its authors, helping to craft their vision throughout each step in the publishing process. Here, art director/graphic artist Michele Scheve (right) works with author/illustrator Amy Tiller on the design for Tiller's book, *My Brother Is Like a Baby Bird*.

photo by thomas s. england

Grateful Steps assists authors with every step to turn their rough ideas into professional publications.

Glass artist Carl Powell (below) is one of the nine professional crafters who rent studio space from the Grovewood Gallery—an off-the-beaten-path Asheville gallery (left) located behind the Grove Park Inn. Powell, a National Endowment for the Arts recipient, is noted for his works in stained glass and sculpted glass. With a process he developed himself, Powell's laminated glass sculptures come alive with multifaceted shapes that form prismatic optical illusions of movement. "The etched images appear to be floating in the piece," he explains.

all photos by mario morgado

THE LOBSTER TRAP: maine courses served with mountain flavor

photo by thomas s. england

▲ The Lobster Trap restaurant treats diners not only to tasty cuisine, but to the talent of local musicians— no cover charge—every night from 7:00 to 9:00 p.m. Here, the Trevor Trio, a jazz band, plays to a full house. "We put a lot of effort into showcasing the many attractions that Asheville has to offer," says Amy Beard, owner. While patrons enjoyed jazz on this night, tomorrow might bring bluegrass or the blues.

Whether you're craving lobster and crab fresh from the New England coastline or mouthwatering trout from a mountain stream, the Lobster Trap restaurant in Asheville provides a menu brimming with delicacies for seafarers and land lovers alike. This restaurant is a dream realized for owner/operator Amy Beard, who yearned for a career that would keep her in touch with two worlds—her native Maine and the Blue Ridge Mountains.

Beard, her staff, lifelong friend and Maine fisherman Captain Tom, and world-class Chef Tres achieve the vision by combining the seafood delicacies of Maine with the savory flavors of Appalachian recipes. "We certainly sell more lobster than I thought we would in the middle of the mountains," said Beard, speaking of the best seller on the menu. That lobster is transported directly from Captain Tom's traps and flown by U.S. Cargo directly to Asheville three times per week.

The unique fare, weekly specials, live local musicians, and a choice of eighty premium wines entice both locals and tourists. Beard shows the community her appreciation by purchasing all produce and trout locally, and the restaurant's interior was completely renovated and decorated by the city's artisans. As the jingle by Chef Tres states: We're here to fulfill your seafood fantasy. ❖

When you're at the place
That you can go
For music, fresh fish, and a cooking show
You must be where the mountain meets the sea.

The Lobster Trap restaurant in Asheville provides a menu brimming with delicacies for seafarers and land lovers alike.

Unless they check out the historic artifacts on display, few visitors to the lobby of the Doubletree Biltmore Hotel realize they are actually in what was once part of the ice-cream manufacturing area of Biltmore Dairy Farms. Owned by the farsighted George W. Vanderbilt, the company's name was synonymous with the very best milk and ice cream available at the beginning of 1900. A closer look at the colorful ice-cream molds and old-time dairy gear tell the story of how one of Asheville's leading hotels came to be.

photo by alan s. weiner

PROGRESS ENERGY — it's all about balance

photo by scott indermaur

▲ Progress Energy's commitment to a cleaner environment and better community can be seen in the large white plumes rising from its cleanstack. The utility company serves more than 150,000 customers in Western North Carolina.

The large white plumes rising from the cleanstack at Progress Energy's Asheville Steam Electric Plant are a constant reminder of the importance of balance in Western North Carolina. In this case, balance means the relationship of providing reliable electric power to more than 150,000 households and businesses in the region with environmental stewardship.

In 2002, North Carolina passed groundbreaking legislation called the Clean Smokestacks Act. This legislation paved the way for electric utilities to invest in the latest emission-control technologies to improve air quality. Many individuals, environmental groups, and elected officials from Asheville were leaders in the cooperative effort with utilities.

As a result, in December 2005, Progress Energy's Asheville Plant became the first power plant in North Carolina to begin operating technologies to reduce emissions under the legislation. These technologies (flue-gas desulfurization, or "scrubbers," and selective-catalytic reduction) have reduced sulfur dioxide (SO_2) and nitrogen oxide (NO_x) emissions each by 93 percent over baseline years. In addition, mercury emissions have been lowered by approximately 80 percent, making this one of the cleanest coal-fired power plants in the country.

Scrubbers convert SO_2 emissions into gypsum and water vapor. The water vapor is released from the stacks as visible "white clouds," while the gypsum is recycled in the manufacture of construction products such as wallboard and cement.

Not only does Progress Energy balance the generation of electricity with a healthy environment, but it also works to develop balanced solutions for our energy future. Thus, in addition to traditional methods of generating electricity, the energy solutions of the future will include renewable technologies that are proven to be environment-friendly, reliable, and cost-effective. And to help offset higher energy demands driven by growth and consumer preferences, Progress Energy offers incentives for green-building efficiencies, energy conservation, and demand-side management controls, and encourages customers to use energy wisely.

Progress Energy also balances its responsibility as a for-profit, regulated enterprise with a tradition of involvement and investment in the community. Between 2002 and 2006, Progress Energy contributed more than $3.7 million locally to support economic development, the environment, education, and community organizations. Additionally, employees give generously of their time and money to local causes. Whether they are wielding hammers for Habitat for Humanity, answering phones for the Pediatric Brain Tumor Foundation's radiothon, or digging deep into their pockets to support low-income families through the company's Energy Neighbor Fund, employees know the importance of giving back.

That community involvement is a natural extension of the commitment that Progress Energy employees have for "keeping the lights on" reliably and safely. In fact, Progress Energy has been recognized more than any U.S. utility by the Edison Electric Institute for superlative efforts to restore electric service after major storms, whether in the company's service area or in support of other utilities. Progress Energy was the first utility to win the J.D. Power & Associates Founders Award for dedication, commitment, and sustained improvement in customer service. And in 2006, the company received the prestigious Edison Award, the top honor among U.S. investor-owned utility companies, for outstanding achievements in operational performance, reliability, customer service, and environmental stewardship. ❖

▲ Progress Energy employees are dedicated to giving back to our communities. They actively support organizations and programs that focus on improving the quality of life that makes Western North Carolina a great place to live and work for everyone.

photo by scott indermaur

Progress Energy offers incentives for green-building efficiencies, and encourages customers to use energy wisely.

photo by mario morgado

photo by mario morgado

FIRST BAPTIST CHVRCH

Sacred places welcome all to worship.

Asheville has long been a place of healing and faith. From landmark buildings with towering steeples to small rural churches, almost every architectural style is represented. The region's diversity of worship is captured in a sampling of denominations serving local congregations. The Basilica of St. Lawrence (far left) not only serves its Catholic congregation with daily masses, it is also one of the city's most beautiful and historic buildings. The First Baptist Church is noted for its creative and uplifting services, accompanied by exceptional choral and instrumental music. Built by George Vanderbilt as the parish church for the village adjacent to the Biltmore House, the Cathedral of All Souls still fulfills its original mission connecting all peoples in the region with faith. Other congregations in the region include Methodist, Eastern Orthodox, Pentecostal, Mennonite, Lutheran, Episcopal, Jewish, Covenant, Presbyterian, Anglican, Holiness, Apostolic, Christian Scientist, Nazarene, Jesus Christ of Latter-day Saints, Church of Christ, and Assembly of God.

The Cathedral of All Souls
Episcopal Diocese of Western North Carolina
Consecrated 1896
Listed in the National Register of Historic Places

photo by thomas s. england

HOMETRUST BANK: financial partner, community booster

At every one of Hometrust Bank's seven branches, in and around Asheville, you'll find the same selection of big-bank products and services matched with the warmth and personal caring only a community bank can offer.

photo by scott indermaur

Since our establishment in 1926, HomeTrust Bank has grown into the largest bank in North Carolina, with more than $1 billion in assets. While our size allows us to offer big-bank products and services, we have retained that culture of warmth and personal caring that only a community bank can deliver.

From the start, we have understood that by financing home ownership, we would help our communities thrive. Visit any of our retail banks today, conveniently located throughout our region, and you'll find a number of services geared toward helping customers buy their own home.

We also offer a growing array of commercial services to help your business run more effectively. Yet our greatest financial tool may well be our bankers themselves—people who care about building relationships and who have the experience to help you map out a successful financial plan.

As for personal banking, we believe it should be, well, personal. That's why you'll find so many flexible options in the types of accounts and services we offer. Whether you're a college student starting out or a retiree managing investments, you'll find an account that fits your lifestyle.

We are a mutually owned bank, strongly rooted in our communities with a heritage of working hard to make neighborhoods stronger and safer. A safety net, a helping hand, a hometown booster—we believe this is what it means to be a true community bank. ✧

We have retained that culture of warmth and personal caring that only a community bank can deliver.

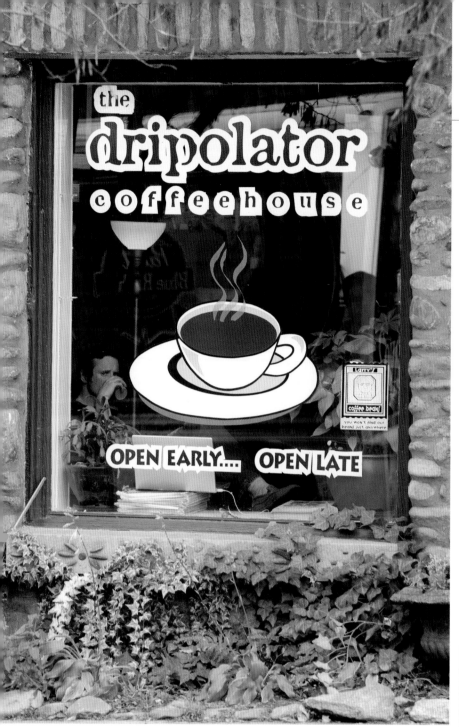

(left)

Whether in downtown Asheville or nearby Black Mountain, the Dripolator Coffeehouse is a great place to stop in for breakfast, lunch, dessert, or just some of the best coffee and teas around. The shops, which are favorite hangouts of their respective locals, also feature free wireless zones.

(below)

After performing at the Wednesday West Asheville Tailgate market, Judith Zander and John Ferris, known otherwise as the musical duo Bee & Boo, popped in next door at the co-op for something to quench their thirst. The Haywood Road Market co-op stocks mostly locally grown organic produce, as well as products from craftspeople and artisans in the area. Located in the renovated Blesdoe Building in West Asheville, the co-op is one of the businesses credited with rejuvenating the Haywood Road commercial corridor.

ROBERTS & STEVENS: a firm dedicated to its founding state

Employees of Roberts & Stevens, here poised for action, adopted College Street as their monthly Adopt-A-Street cleanup program. This is one of many community outreaches with which this Asheville-based law firm is involved, including the Girl and Boy Scouts, Big Brothers, Big Sisters, the Manna Food Bank, Mission Hospital, the Asheville Area Chamber of Commerce, Pack Place, and the Golden Leaf Foundation.

photo by alan s. weiner

From their offices in the BB&T Building towering over downtown Asheville, Roberts & Stevens lawyers command a view of the area—Asheville, Buncombe County, and beyond to the west and to the east. The view reflects the firm's goal to be the law firm of choice from Interstate 77 west to Murphy. In the words of John S. "Jack" Stevens, cofounder, the view represents their focus as lawyers—to serve the city and the surrounding region.

Founded in 1986 as the product of a merger between two old Asheville firms, Roberts & Stevens takes its name from Landon Roberts and Jack Stevens. Landon Roberts, a native of Madison County, attended Mars Hill College and the University of North Carolina at Chapel Hill. Following service in the Pacific Theatre in World War II, he obtained his law degree from UNC and practiced law in Asheville from 1948 until his death at age eighty-five, in 2007. Jack Stevens, of Buncombe County, also attended UNC–Chapel Hill with an interruption for service in the U.S. Army. Together, Roberts and Stevens built the firm, which now consists of twenty-six lawyers.

The firm provides a broad range of legal services, including health care, education, business and corporate, estate and probate, real estate, litigation, bankruptcy, governmental, and environmental. Well-earned recognition includes Best Lawyers in America, and membership in the North Carolina Legal Elite and North Carolina Super Lawyers. With a reputation driven by a commitment to excellence, Roberts & Stevens lawyers contribute to their community, their clients, and their state. ❖

The view represents their focus as lawyers—to serve the city and the surrounding region.

photo by rod reilly

At Hickory Nut Gorge and along the road to Black Mountain near Asheville, travelers can always find one-of-a-kind shopping opportunities. Plan on not being able to resist the roadside stands and stores serving up crafts, regional art, clothing, and that unique element called southern hospitality from residents such as Kayla Corn of Bat Cave, North Carolina, shown here at the Old Cider Mill and Gift Shop.

Two young girls enjoy time in the autumn sun during the annual Harvest Celebration at the Biltmore Estate. Held on the grounds of the magnificent former home of George Vanderbilt, the event is a celebration of the area's Appalachian heritage.

ASHEVILLE PATRON

Strauss & Associates, P.A.
ESTATE PLANNING ATTORNEYS

STRAUSS & ASSOCIATES — planning your legacy

From offices in Asheville and Hendersonville, the Strauss & Associates law firm provides clients in Western North Carolina with estate planning, asset protection, and business succession planning. The firm's estate planning services include wills, trusts, estate tax planning, Medicaid eligibility planning, charitable planning, and administration of and probating of assets in the event of death or incompetency. In protecting assets, the firm works to safeguard assets from marital disputes or lawsuits. And in business succession planning, the firm helps clients with successful exit strategies that include transfer of the company to existing employees, family members, or third parties. Strauss & Associates' five attorneys include Florida and North Carolina lawyers board-certified as specialists in estate planning and in elder law.

77 Central Avenue, Suite F
Asheville, North Carolina 28801
828.258.0994
www.strausslaw.com

ASHEVILLE FEATURED COMPANIES

The Alpha Group
84 Coxe Avenue, Suite 1-B
Asheville, North Carolina 28801
828.258.9553
www.thealphagroup.com

advertising agency *(pp. 148–149)*
From nationally known clients to local businesses, the Alpha Group brings advertising to Asheville, North Carolina, in a universal way. With a professional staff gathered from around the nation and the world, this small business delivers with big-business impact. Every client can expect only the best in terms of audience identification and the perfect choice of media messaging.

Asheville Area Chamber of Commerce
36 Montford Avenue
Asheville, North Carolina 28801
828-258-6101
www.ashevillechamber.org

chamber of commerce *(pp. 38–39)*
The Asheville Area Chamber of Commerce is a partnership of over two thousand businesses, organizations, and coalitions supporting the community and each other. The Chamber consists of various departments with different funding and focuses, including tourism, economic development, member services, public policy, and workforce development.

Asheville-Buncombe Technical Community College

340 Victoria Road
Asheville, North Carolina 28801
828.254.1921
www.abtech.edu

school – university *(pp. 224–225)*

A-B Tech, founded in 1959, offers more than fifty innovative career programs, along with college transfer degrees and more than twelve hundred continuing education courses. A-B Tech has three campuses in Buncombe and Madison counties.

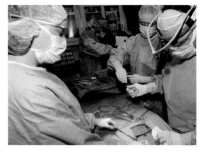

Asheville Cabins of Willow Winds

39 Stockwood Road Extension
Asheville, North Carolina 28803
828.277.0254
www.willowwinds.com

lodging – resort cabins *(pp. 172–175)*

Asheville Cabins of Willow Winds is a thirty-nine-acre resort property conveniently located within the city limits of Asheville and five minutes from the entrance to Biltmore Estate. Bordered by the Blue Ridge Parkway and the Mountains-to-the-Sea Trail, Willow Winds features twenty-five well-appointed log and cedar cabins that provide access to a unique balance between nature's tranquility and Asheville's exciting attractions.

Asheville Citizen-Times

14 O. Henry Avenue
Asheville, North Carolina 28801
828.232.5934
www.citizen-times.com

media – newspaper *(p. 56)*

The *Asheville Citizen-Times* is a Gannett newspaper. Along with that daily newspaper, the publishing company prints several regional and weekly community newspapers. Citizen-Times.com is the most visited site in the region, averaging 5 million page views and 388,000 unique visitors per month.

Asheville Renaissance Hotel

One Thomas Wolfe Plaza
Asheville, North Carolina 28801
828.210.3009
www.ashevillerenaissance.com

hotel *(pp. 212–213)*

With 275 guest rooms, six suites, and approximately twenty thousand square feet of total meeting space, the twelve-story Asheville Renaissance Hotel has become a top choice for business and pleasure travelers to the Asheville area. Its central location also puts guests within minutes of the best downtown Asheville has to offer: fine dining, wonderful art galleries, and a host of historic attractions.

Asheville Vein Center & Medical Spa

131 McDowell Street
Suite 300
Asheville, North Carolina 28801
828.350.1580
www.ashevilleveincenter.com

health care – physician group *(pp. 162–164)*

One of the leading vein centers in the country, Asheville Vein Center & Medical Spa specializes in minimally invasive varicose vein laser surgery and spider vein treatment, and also offers an array of preventative and corrective skin-care treatments under the care of surgical specialists.

BH Commercial, a Division of Beverly-Hanks & Associates

410 Executive Park
Asheville, North Carolina 28801
866.810.5893 (toll free)
www.bhcommercial.com

real estate – commercial *(pp. 46–47)*

BH Commercial is a division of Beverly-Hanks & Associates, the largest real estate firm in Western North Carolina. A full-service brokerage firm, BH Commercial offers sales and marketing services for industrial, warehouse, multifamily, retail, and office properties; land acquisition; leasing administration; and real estate investment consultation. The BH Commercial Team also represents buyers and tenants in the search for appropriate commercial properties.

Beverly-Hanks & Associates

300 Executive Park
Asheville, North Carolina 28801
866.858.2257
www.beverly-hanks.com

real estate *(pp. 80–84)*

Beverly-Hanks & Associates is the largest real estate firm in Western North Carolina. The firm has more than three hundred sales associates and seven office locations in Buncombe, Henderson, and Haywood counties. Its services include residential sales of new and existing homes, commercial brokerage services, builder and developer marketing services, relocation assistance, and mortgage services.

Beverly-Hanks Mortgage Services

300 Executive Park
Asheville, North Carolina 28801
866.858.2257
www.BHmortgageservices.com

mortgage services *(pp. 120–121)*

Beverly-Hanks Mortgage Services is the financing arm of Beverly-Hanks & Associates, the largest real estate firm in Western North Carolina. In addition to a full range of residential and commercial loan products, Beverly-Hanks Mortgage Services staffs six of the firm's seven offices with dedicated loan officers and offers appointments outside regular office hours.

Biltmore Estate

One North Pack Square
Asheville, North Carolina 28801
828.225.1333 or 1-877-Biltmore
www.biltmore.com

attraction *(pp. 102–103)*

In addition to being the palatial home of George Vanderbilt, American's largest private residence, and a National Historic Landmark, the Biltmore Co. is now a national brand, which sells its collection of home and garden products through three thousand retail locations. Biltmore has also added a winery, a luxury hotel, five restaurants, a number of tours, and a dozen shops on the estate grounds.

Biltmore Farms Commercial

One Town Square Boulevard
Suite 330
Asheville, North Carolina 28803
828.210.1667
www.biltmorefarmscommercial.com

real estate – developer *(p. 106)*

Biltmore Farms Commercial offers a wide range of leasing and sales services for property owners, prospective investors, and companies that are considering owning or leasing real property. The company combines an aggressive leasing program with a relationship-driven property services team dedicated to tenant retention, safety, and efficiency.

Biltmore Farms Communities

One Town Square Boulevard
Suite 330
Asheville, North Carolina 28803
828.210.1667
www.biltmorefarms.com

real estate – developer *(p. 108)*

George W. Vanderbilt's commitment to maintaining the natural beauty and quality of life in Western North Carolina is evident in each of the Biltmore Farms Communities, which include Biltmore Forest, Biltmore Park®, Biltmore Lake®, as well as the newest residential development, The Ramble℠.

Biltmore Farms Homes

One Town Square Boulevard
Suite 330
Asheville, North Carolina 28803
828.210.1667
www.mybiltmorehome.com

real estate – developer *(p. 110)*

Biltmore Farms Homes give homeowners the opportunity to live in a home built to the same level of excellence George Vanderbilt called for in his home. Each home is designed for lifelong comfort inside and out. Exterior styles, ranging from French to English, Craftsman to Classical, are the perfect complement to the beauty of the Blue Ridge Mountains.

Biltmore Farms Hotels

One Town Square Boulevard, Suite 330
Asheville, North Carolina 28803
www.biltmorefarmshotels.com

Doubletree Biltmore

15 Hendersonville Road
Asheville, North Carolina 28803
828.771.2271
www.biltmorefarmshotels.com

Biltmore Farms, LLC

One Town Square Boulevard
Suite 330
Asheville, North Carolina 28803
828.210.1667
www.biltmorefarms.com

Blue Ridge Limousine

54 North Willow Brook Drive
Asheville, North Carolina 28806
828.232.4046
www.blueridgelimo.com

Bruisin' Ales

66 Broadway Street, Suite 1
Asheville, North Carolina 28801
828.252.8999
www.bruisin-ales.com

Carolina Day School

1345 Hendersonville Road
Asheville, North Carolina 28803
828.274.0757
www.cdschool.org

Carolina First Bank

22 South Pack Square
Suite 503
Asheville, North Carolina 28801
828.255.0693
www.carolinafirst.com

hotels *(pp. 90–91)*

The Doubletree Biltmore Hotel, a member of the Hilton chain, is managed by Biltmore Farms Hotels, which also manages Quality Inn and Suites Biltmore South, Residence Inn Biltmore, and Sleep Inn Biltmore. Each of its 160 well-appointed, comfortable rooms reflects the gracious hospitality originally shown by George W. Vanderbilt to his guests at Biltmore.

real estate – developer *(pp. 112–113)*

Biltmore Farms represents a diverse array of companies, each serving an essential function in building the Western North Carolina community. Including hospitality, residential, retail and commercial development, and new-home construction, each Biltmore Farms company is committed to the values of stewardship, quality, and integrity that are synonymous with its namesake, George Vanderbilt.

limousine company *(pp. 228–229)*

Established in 2003 on a small budget and with one vehicle, Blue Ridge Limousine has grown to become Asheville's premier ground transportation company with a fleet of seven vehicles, including one that runs on biodiesel. Whether you're a local businessperson or a high school student, a visiting celebrity or presidential candidate, Blue Ridge will ensure your ground transportation experience is one of luxury and comfort.

retail – specialty beer *(pp. 130–131)*

Bruisin' Ales is a specialty beer store located in historical downtown Asheville. Opened in late 2006 by proprietors and self-proclaimed "beerlanthropists" Jason and Julie Atallah, the shop features more than 450 beers, including Belgians, Belgian-style, high-gravity, craft brews, microbrews, and the very best available beers from around the world.

school – private *(pp. 134–136)*

Working in partnership with parents, Asheville's premier comprehensive independent school challenges young people to pursue their personal quest for excellence by engaging them in a rigorous, college preparatory program and offering them opportunities to educate the mind, the heart, the body, and the human spirit.

bank *(pp. 166–169)*

A subsidiary of the South Financial Group, Carolina First Bank, in Asheville, North Carolina, offers big-bank services with hometown responsiveness. Business owners and individuals alike enjoy the bank's capacity to make decisions at the local level with the financial power of a multistate financial institution.

City of Asheville
P.O. Box 7148
70 Court Plaza
Asheville, North Carolina 28802
828.251.1122
www.ashevillenc.gov

government – city *(pp. 116–117)*
The City of Asheville works with residents to ensure that the community retains its renowned quality of life and remains a regional hub for business, health care, culture, dining, and entertainment.

Deerfield Episcopal Retirement Community
1617 Hendersonville Road
Asheville, North Carolina 28803
828.274.1531
800.284.1531
www.deerfieldwnc.org

retirement community *(pp. 216–217)*
The mission of Deerfield Episcopal Retirement Community is to operate a nonprofit retirement community guided by Christian ideals, to offer a continuum of care to all people, to promote independence and the highest quality of life, and to provide physical and financial security.

Dixon Hughes PLLC
500 Ridgefield Court
Asheville, North Carolina 28806
828.254.2254
www.dixon-hughes.com

CPA firm *(pp. 70–72)*
Dixon Hughes is the largest accounting/consulting firm headquartered in the Southeast. Through organic growth and a series of strategic mergers, the firm now has more than one thousand employees and over twenty offices, serving clients locally, nationally, and internationally.

George W. Morosani & Associates
932 Hendersonville Road
Asheville, North Carolina 28803
828-274-4111
www.morosani.com

real estate – commercial *(pp. 94–96)*
Morosani & Associates has served Western North Carolina with commercial, industrial, and residential properties and property management since 1969. The company brokers, leases, and manages commercial real estate for investors while maintaining an extensive inventory of retail and office space, undeveloped land, multipurpose buildings, and business rentals.

Givens Estates
2360 Sweeten Creek Road
Asheville, North Carolina 28803
828.771.2625
www.givensestates.com

retirement community *(pp. 208–209)*
Givens Estates United Methodist Retirement Community offers seniors a place to lead active, fulfilling lives by encouraging wellness in all aspects of daily living. The community is open to all income levels, offers over four hundred residences in a wide range of floor plans, and features a full complement of amenities and a full continuum of health-care services.

Gould Killian CPA Group, PA
100 Coxe Avenue
Asheville, North Carolina 28801
823.258-0363
www.gk-cpa.com

Altamont Capital Management, LLC
100 Coxe Avenue
Asheville, North Carolina 28801
823.236.0610

cpa firm – investment *(p. 190)*
Defined by a teamwork approach, steady growth, and stable long-term client relationships, Gould Killian and Altamont provide clients with personalized, comprehensive services including accounting, consulting, tax, audit, and financial advisory services.

Grateful Steps

1091 Hendersonville Road
Asheville, North Carolina 28803
828.277.0998
www.gratefulsteps.com

book publisher *(p. 232)*

Is there a book inside you? A story you'd like to tell, an idea you want to bring to light? Grateful Steps, a full-service book publishing company serving individuals, businesses, and churches in Western North Carolina, will help guide you through the process.

Groce Funeral Home

1401 Patton Avenue
Asheville, North Carolina 28806
828.252.3535
www.grocefuneralhome.com

funeral home – mortuary *(pp. 186–188)*

Groce Funeral Home was founded in 1929 by the sons of Rev. T. A. Groce, one of the last circuit-riding Methodist ministers traveling in the mountains of Western North Carolina. It is still a local, family business, involving the third generation, Bill and his brother Dale, and the fourth generation, Scott and W. H. ("Trey") Groce. Due to their reputation for integrity and the efforts of a dedicated staff, Groce Funeral Home has become Buncombe County's largest funeral service provider.

The Grove Park Inn Resort & Spa

290 Macon Avenue
Asheville, North Carolina 28804
828.252.2711
www.groveparkinn.com

hotel – resort *(p. 140)*

Built in 1913 in the scenic Blue Ridge foothills, the Grove Park Inn continues to serve as an elegant respite from the outside world. Today, it ranks among the top-ten spa destinations in the world, attracting clientele who enjoy the best in rejuvenating treatments, indoor and outdoor activities, fine dining, luxury accommodations, and legendary service.

HomeTrust Bank

P.O. Box 10
Asheville, North Carolina 28802
828.350.3062
www.hometrustbanking.com

bank *(p. 240)*

HomeTrust Bank is one of four hometown banks to form the HomeTrust Banking Partnership, bringing customers big-bank home, commercial, and personal banking products and services, matched with the warmth and personal care only a community bank can offer.

Insurance Service of Asheville

408 Executive Park, Building 3
Asheville, North Carolina 28801
828.253.1668
www.isa-avl.com

insurance company *(pp. 98–99)*

Insurance Service of Asheville (ISA) is a full-service, multilines insurance agency offering everything from commercial lines and personal coverage to life, health, and employee benefits. ISA caters to the various needs of individuals, families, and businesses throughout the region.

Jewels That Dance

63 Haywood Street
Asheville, North Carolina 28801
828.254.5088
www.jewelsthatdance.com

retail – jewelry store *(pp. 178–179)*

Jewels That Dance is Asheville's finest jewelry gallery and design studio. Founded in 1983, it now represents more than fifty designers producing one-of-a-kind rings, bracelets, pendants, necklaces, engagement rings, and wedding bands using platinum, gold, titanium, sterling, diamonds, fine gemstones, and pearls.

Johnson, Price & Sprinkle PA
79 Woodfin Place
Suite 300
Asheville, North Carolina 28801
828.254.2374
www.jpspa.com

CPA firm *(pp. 182–183)*
Johnson, Price & Sprinkle PA is a regional certified public accounting firm that offers a variety of tax and financial planning, management, and consulting services to their clients through three Western North Carolina locations in Asheville, Hendersonville, and Marion.

Kimmel & Associates
25 Page Avenue
Asheville, North Carolina 28801
828.251.9900
www.kimmel.com

executive search firm *(pp. 24-27)*
Kimmel & Associates, which has been in Asheville more than twenty-five years, is the largest executive search firm in the nation specializing in the construction industry. Working with a staff of professional recruiters and consultants, the company places an average of thirteen hundred candidates with top companies each year.

The Lobster Trap
35 Patton Avenue
Asheville, North Carolina 28801
828.350.0505
www.thelobstertrap.biz

restaurant *(p. 234)*
The Lobster Trap restaurant in Asheville opened its doors in 2005, and hungry customers have been flooding in ever since. With live music, a fun atmosphere, a choice of eighty wines, and a menu that combines fresh Maine seafood with mountain fare, the establishment enjoys repeat appearances from satisfied customers (locals and tourists) throughout the year.

McGuire, Wood & Bissette, P.A.
48 Patton Avenue
Asheville, North Carolina 28801
828.254.8800
www.mwbavl.com

law firm *(pp. 52–53)*
For more than a century, the law firm of McGuire, Wood & Bissette, P.A., has provided a wealth of expertise and quality legal work for business, industry, and families throughout Western North Carolina. The core of the firm's philosophy is a set of shared values that influence how each client matter is handled: with integrity, honesty, and enjoyment of the work at hand. These values result in solutions that comprehensively meet clients' business and legal challenges.

Mission Health & Hospitals
345 Biltmore Avenue
Asheville, North Carolina 28801
828.213.4802
www.missionhospitals.org

Asheville Cardiology Associates
P.O. Box 7239
Asheville, North Carolina 28802
828.274-6000
www.avlcard.com

Asheville Cardiovascular and Thoracic Surgeons
257 McDowell Street
Asheville, North Carolina 28803
828.258.1121
www.avlcvsurgeons.com

hospital – medical center *(pp. 192–194)*
Mission Health & Hospitals is the regional referral center for Western North Carolina and the adjoining region. In Asheville, Mission resides on two across-the-street campuses, Memorial and St. Joseph. It also includes Blue Ridge Regional Hospital in Mitchell and Yancey counties and the McDowell Hospital in McDowell County. The multihospital system is not-for-profit and has received numerous national quality awards.

Mountain Air Country Club
P.O. Box 1037
Burnsville, North Carolina 28714
800.247.7791
www.mountainaircc.com

residential and golf community *(pp. 142–145)*
Mountain Air Country Club is an award-winning thirteen-hundred-acre private mountaintop golf community located in the North Carolina Blue Ridge Mountains just thirty-five minutes northeast of Asheville. It features homesites that range from $400,000 to more than $2 million, condominium homes from $399,000 to more than $4 million, and custom homes from $650,000 to more than $5 million. In addition to breathtaking views of the surrounding mountains and a two-thousand-foot-deep valley, it offers unparalleled amenities, including a championship eighteen-hole golf course, tennis courts, swimming pool, clubhouse, and a paved private runway.

Padgett & Freeman Architects
30 Choctaw Street
Asheville, North Carolina 28801
828.254.1963
www.padgettandfreeman.com

architect *(pp. 74–75)*
Ingenuity, creativity, and highly personal customer service mark the ongoing success of Padgett & Freeman Architects, PA. Based in Asheville, North Carolina, with a regional client outreach to surrounding areas and states, including Georgia, the firm is known for its diverse capabilities, including planning, architecture, renovation, and interior design.

Plasticard Locktech International
605 Sweeten Creek Industrial Park
Asheville, North Carolina 28803
800.752.1017
www.plicards.com

manufacturing company *(pp. 152–155)*
Plasticard Locktech International (PLI) produces hotel key cards for thousands of top-name hospitality clients around the world. The company's products can be tailored to advertise for clients from all industries or to create a treasured memento of any event.

Preferred Properties
39 Woodfin Street
Asheville, North Carolina 28801
828.258.2953
www.preferredprop.com

1075 Hendersonville Road, Suite 100
Biltmore Forest, North Carolina 28803
828.210.9400
www.preferredprop.com

real estate – residential *(pp. 64–66)*
Preferred Properties provides personalized attention to the needs and wishes of homebuyers and sellers. The company has been serving Asheville since 1968 and operates from offices in downtown Asheville and Biltmore Forest.

Progress Energy
555-A Brevard Road
Asheville, North Carolina 28806
828.258.5019
www.progress-energy.com

utility company *(pp. 236–237)*
Progress Energy, headquartered in Raleigh, North Carolina, is a Fortune 250 diversified energy company with more than twenty-three thousand megawatts of generation capacity and $10 billion in annual revenues. The company's holdings include two electric utilities serving approximately 3.1 million customers in North Carolina, South Carolina, and Florida. Its nonregulated operations include energy marketing.

Pulliam Properties Inc.
2 Walden Ridge Drive, Suite 70
Asheville, North Carolina 28803
828.684.4344
www.pulliamproperties.com

real estate – commercial *(pp. 124–127)*
Pulliam Properties Inc. is a family-owned, full-service commercial real estate and development firm. Founded by Winston W. Pulliam in 1982 and purchased by his son Rusty Pulliam in 1993, the company is recognized as one of the leading forces behind the development of Asheville. Today, Pulliam Properties focuses on land development, brokerage/sales, and management, and owns more than seventy properties throughout Asheville totaling 3.5 million square feet of space.

Roberts & Stevens, P.A.
P.O. Box 7647
Asheville, North Carolina 28802
828.252.6600
www.roberts-stevens.com

law firm *(p. 242)*
With a long and respected history of service in Asheville, Roberts & Stevens, P.A., offers a full range of legal services to citizens of the city and the surrounding area. Attorneys with in-depth knowledge of their respective fields and a dedication to clientele make Roberts & Stevens the firm of choice for excellent representation.

Sisters of Mercy Services —— ARP/Phoenix

1201 Patton Avenue
Asheville, North Carolina 28806
828.210.2121
www.somsc.org
www.urgentcares.org
www.arp-phoenix.com

health-care services *(pp. 42-43)*

Sisters of Mercy Services Corporation provides comprehensive health-care services to Buncombe and its surrounding counties. From Sisters of Mercy Urgent Care to ARP/Phoenix, the organization covers a full spectrum of health-care services, from general medical care to substance abuse and behavioral health. In addition, Sisters of Mercy Services ensures that all residents across Western North Carolina have access to affordable, high-quality care through the Compassionate Care Program, a tiered discount process for patients who require financial assistance.

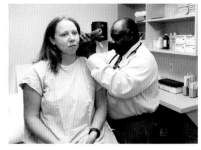

Southern Community Bank and Trust

80 Peachtree Road, Suite 106
Asheville, North Carolina 28803
828.274.7577
www.smallenoughtocare.com

bank *(p. 160)*

Southern Community Bank and Trust, a full-service banking institution, entered the Asheville market in early 2007, offering a wide variety of personal, business, and investor services. Asheville serves as North Carolina's western region headquarters, with new branches being added to the area regularly. The bank trades under the common stock symbol SCMF.

Timothy E. Gillespie, DMD, FAGD

36 Orange Street
Asheville, North Carolina 28801
828.252.9351
www.drtimgillespie.com

cosmetic, implant, and general dentistry *(pp. 30-32)*

In a fun, family-type environment, Timothy E. Gillespie, DMD, FAGD, offers a comprehensive scope of services, from dental checkups and cleanings to cosmetic enhancements and restorative treatments to periodontal disease management and implants for missing teeth.

United Way of Asheville and Buncombe County

50 South French Broad Avenue
Asheville, North Carolina 28801
828.255.0696
www.unitedwayabc.org

nonprofit *(p. 222)*

Caring for neighbors since 1921, the United Way of Asheville and Buncombe County focuses on supporting programs that are relevant to the local population. The organization's staff, volunteers, and generous givers ensure that this United Way agency remains a vibrant, eclectic, efficient, and effective nonprofit that regularly examines and addresses ever-changing community needs.

Western Carolina University

Admissions—102 Camp Building
Cullowhee, North Carolina 28723
828.277.7317
www.wcu.edu

school – university *(p. 206)*

Founded in 1889, Western Carolina University is a member of the University of North Carolina and serves almost nine thousand students. From its main campus in Cullowhee, North Carolina, graduate center at UNC-A, classes at various community colleges throughout the region, and through distance education, WCU offers more than 120 undergraduate and graduate areas of study, including nationally top-ranked entrepreneurship, nursing, and teacher education programs.

Wolf Mountain Realty

383 Wolf Laurel Road
Mars Hill, North Carolina 28754
828.680.9777
www.wolfmountainrealty.com

real estate - residential *(pp. 202-203)*

Since its establishment in 1998, Wolf Mountain Realty has grown into one of the region's premier real estate and property management agencies. It serves clients seeking homes throughout North Carolina and Tennessee and is a top seller of residential homes and vacation rentals in Wolf Laurel Resort.

ASHEVILLE EDITORIAL TEAM

Kimberly Fox DeMeza, Writer, Roswell, Georgia. Combining business insight with creative flair, DeMeza writes to engage the audience as well as communicate the nuances of the subject matter. While officially beginning her career in public relations in 1980 with a degree in journalism, and following in 1990 with a master's in health management, writing has always been central to her professional experience. From speechwriting to corporate brochures to business magazine feature writing, DeMeza enjoys the process of crafting the message. Delving into the topic is simply one of the benefits, as she believes every writing opportunity is an opportunity to continue to learn.

Rena Distasio, Writer, Tijeras, New Mexico. Freelance writer Rena Distasio contributes articles and reviews on a variety of subjects to regional and national publications. She also edits two magazines focused on life in the Four Corners region. In her spare time she and her husband and their dog enjoy the great outdoors from their home in the mountains east of Albuquerque.

Grace Hawthorne, Writer, Atlanta, Georgia. Starting as a reporter, she has written everything from advertising for septic tanks to the libretto for an opera. While in New York, she worked for Time-Life Books and wrote for *Sesame Street*. As a performer, she has appeared at the Carter Presidential Center, Callanwolde Fine Arts Center, and at various corporate functions. Her latest project is a two-woman show called *Pushy Broads and Proper Southern Ladies*.

Amy Meadows, Writer, Canton, Georgia. Meadows is an accomplished feature writer who has been published in a wide variety of local, regional, and national consumer and trade publications since launching her freelance writing career in 2000. She also specializes in producing corporate marketing literature for companies large and small and holds a master's of arts degree in professional writing from Kennesaw State University.

Regina Roths, Writer, Andover, Kansas. Roths has written extensively about business since launching her journalism career in the early 1990s. Her prose can be found in corporate coffee-table books nationwide as well as on regionally produced Web sites, and in print and online magazines, newspapers, and publications. Her love of industry, history, and research gives her a keen insight into writing and communicating a message.

Gail Snyder, Writer, Woodstock, Georgia. Snyder is a writer and editor with twenty years of experience in corporate communications and publishing. She has edited or written articles focusing on corporate management strategies, published articles in a number of trade magazines and journals, and edited both fiction and nonfiction books. Gail enjoys explaining material to an audience in a way that reveals how any subject can be interesting. She earned her bachelor's degree in journalism from Georgia State University, where she went on to complete her master's in communications. Currently she works as a freelance and contract writer and editor.

Tim Barnwell, Photographer, Asheville, North Carolina. Barnwell's career has spanned over twenty-five years as a professional photographer and photography instructor. He has published two books, *The Face of Appalachia: Portraits from the Mountain Farm* and *On Earth's Furrowed Brow: The Appalachian Farm in Photographs*. His work has been included in dozens of group and one-man shows in the United States and abroad. His prints are in the permanent collections of a number of museums, including the Metropolitan Museum, the New Orleans Museum of Art, and the High Museum in Atlanta. You can see more of his work at www.barnwellphoto.com.

Thomas S. England, Photographer, Decatur, Georgia. England graduated from Northwestern University, and began photography as a newspaper photographer in the Chicago area. He started freelancing for *People* magazine in 1974. Since then he has taken assignments from national magazines and corporations, specializing in photographing people on location. He lives in Decatur, Georgia, with Nancy Foster, a home renovator, and their dog Chessey. More of his photographs may be viewed online at www.englandphoto.com.

Scott Indermaur, Photographer, East Greenwich, Rhode Island. Indermaur's assignments have taken him from the smallest rural communities to the world's most urban environments. His gift lies in discovering the familiar in the exotic and the remarkable in the ordinary. Whether he's capturing a fleeting moment in history or cutting to the essence of a portrait, Scott tells the story in a language everyone understands. When not photographing, Scott—who along with his wife, daughter, and son are all Tae Kwon Do black belts—also enjoys wonderful food and wine, meeting new people, traveling, music, and sailing. You can view his images and contact him at www.siphotography.com.

Mario Morgado, Photographer, Greenwich, Connecticut. Morgado was born in Cuba and somehow managed to have a happy childhood while growing up in Elizabeth, New Jersey. He spent his formative years at the Guggenheim Museum and the right-field bleachers of Yankee Stadium. His work has appeared in numerous publications including *The New York Times*, *Vermont Life*, *New York* magazine, and *Boston* magazine. Mario's work can be seen at www.mariomorgado.com.

Rod Reilly, Photographer, Atlanta, Georgia. Since 1979 Reilly has used his training at Carnegie Mellon School of Design and Rochester Institute of Technology to create compelling environmental portraits on location of people as they live and work. His clients include Home Depot, Coca-Cola USA, United Parcel Service, Cox Communications, and McGraw-Hill. Starting his career as a staff shooter for Georgia Pacific, Rod has owned his own studio, Reilly Arts & Letters, for the last twelve years, and travels often on assignment. He is a member of ASMP and the father of three. His work can be seen at www.rodreillyphoto.com.

Alan S. Weiner, Photographer, Portland, Oregon. Weiner travels extensively both in the United States and abroad. Over the last twenty-three years his work has appeared regularly in *The New York Times*. In addition, his pictures have been published in *USA Today* and in *Time*, *Newsweek*, *Life*, and *People* magazines. He has shot corporate work for IBM, Pepsi, UPS, and other companies large and small. He is also the cofounder of the Wedding Bureau (www.weddingbureau.com). Alan has worked in every region of the country for Riverbend Books. His strengths are in photojournalism.

about the publisher

ASHEVILLE — A Photographic Portrait was published by Bookhouse Group, Inc., under its imprint of Riverbend Books. What many people don't realize is that in addition to picture books on American communities, we also develop and publish institutional histories, commemorative books of all types, contemporary books, and others for clients across the country.

Bookhouse has developed various types of books for prep schools from Utah to Florida, colleges and universities, country clubs, a phone company in Vermont, a church in Atlanta, hospitals, banks, and many other entities. We've also published a catalog for an art collection for a gallery in Texas, a picture book for a worldwide Christian ministry, and a book on a priceless collection of art and antiques for the Atlanta History Center.

These beautiful and treasured tabletop books are developed by our staff as turnkey projects, thus making life easier for the client. If your company has an interest in our publishing services, do not hesitate to contact us.

Founded in 1989, Bookhouse Group is headquartered in a renovated 1920s tobacco warehouse in downtown Atlanta. If you're ever in town, we'd be delighted if you looked us up. Thank you for making possible the publication of ASHEVILLE — A Photographic Portrait.

BOOKHOUSE
GROUP, INC.
www.bookhouse.net

Banks ◇ Prep Schools ◇ Hospitals ◇ Insurance Companies ◇ Art Galleries ◇ Museums
◇ Utilities ◇ Country Clubs ◇ Colleges ◇ Churches ◇ Military Academies ◇ Associations

photo by rod reilly

Each time the lights go up on another production by the Asheville Ballet, the audience knows it is in for a treat. The Asheville Ballet is Western North Carolina's year-round resident company. Supported by the Asheville Ballet Guild Inc. (ABG), the company is committed to creating new works, re-creating worthy existing works—like this production of *Porgy and Bess*—and promoting dance in the region. An innovative twist to this production was the live performance of a jazz band and vocalists. Created in 1963, the ABG is one of the region's oldest nonprofit arts organizations.